Effective Business Writing

Effective Business Writing

JENNIFER MACLENNAN

Prentice-Hall Canada Inc.,
Scarborough, Ontario

Canadian Cataloguing in Publication Data

MacLennan, Jennifer
  Effective business writing

Includes index.
ISBN 0-13-241498-8

1. Business writing. I. Title.

HF5718.3.M24 1989   808'.066651   C89-094294-3

Prentice-Hall, Inc., Englewood Cliffs, New Jersey
Prentice-Hall Internations, Inc., London
Prentice-Hall of Australia, Pty., Ltd., Sydney
Prentice-Hall of India Pvt., Ltd., New Delhi
Prentice-Hall of Japan, Inc., Tokyo
Prentice-Hall of Southeast Asia (Pte.) Ltd., Singapore
Editora Prentice-Hall do Brasil Ltda., Rio de Janeiro
Prentice-Hall Hispanoamericana, S.A., Mexico

ISBN 0-13-241498-8

Production Editor: Maryrose O'Neill
Production Coordinator: Sandra Paige
Text Design: Robert Garbutt Productions

1 2 3 4 5 I.G.   94 93 92 91 90

Printed and bound in Canada by Gagné Printing Ltd.

Table of Contents

Preface   *ix*

1

Style in Business Writing — An Overview   *2*
STEP ONE   Identifying the Main Point / 3
STEP TWO   Identifying Your Reader / 4
STEP THREE   The Six C's of Business Writing / 5

THINGS TO TRY / 11

2

Sharpening Your Business Writing Style   *14*
Preparing to Write / 14
Common Faults of Business Writing / 16

THINGS TO TRY / 20

3

Business Letters and Memos   *27*
Good News and Bad News Messages / 29
Congratulations or Acknowledgement / 29
Complaint / 31
Sales or Persuasive Messages / 33
Refusals / 34

The Parts of a Business Letter / 36
The Parts of a Memo / 41
Letter and Memo Format / 43

THINGS TO TRY / 50

4 Informal Reports 62

The Parts of a Report / 62
    Report Situations / 66
Informal Report Styles / 67
    Report Forms / 69
    Informal Reports / 69
    Sample Informal Report / 72
    Semiformal Reports / 74

THINGS TO TRY / 80

5 Formal Reports and Proposals 86

The Parts of a Formal Report / 86
Using Visuals in a Formal Report / 89
Proposals / 95
Sample Formal Report / 96

THINGS TO TRY / 115

6 Oral Reports and Presentations 119

Types of Oral Presentations / 120
Delivery / 121
    Visible Factors: The Sight of Your Presentation / 121
    Audible Factors: The Sound of Your Presentation / 123
Preparing Your Presentation / 124
Preparing a Business Brief / 127

Visual Aids in Oral Presentations / 129
    Guidelines for the Use of Visual Aids / 129
The Importance of Practice / 130

THINGS TO TRY / 132

7   **The Job Package**   *133*

The Resume / *133*
    Types of Resumes / 134
    Parts of a Resume / 135
    Resume Format / 140
Sample Resumes / 145
The Letter of Application / *168*
    Types of Application Letters / 168
    Appeal to the Employer! / 168
    Sample Letters of Application / 169
The Application Form / *172*
The Letter of Recommendation / *177*
The Job Interview / *181*
    Appearance/First Impressions / 181
    Attitude / 183
    Knowledge / 183
    Employers' Questions / 184
    Some Reasons Why People Don't Get Hired / 188
    What to Expect / 189
    Problem Questions / 190

THINGS TO TRY / 191

Index   *203*

Preface

Any project as complex and demanding as writing a textbook is rarely the effort of one person alone; instead, it reflects the contributions of many people who have offered encouragement, support, and helpful advice. I would like to thank those people whose contributions to my life and work can be seen in this book.

First I wish to acknowledge some gifted teachers who, by advice and example, have helped shape my teaching style and thus the approach I have taken in *Effective Business Writing:* Myron Meikle, Barry Urquhart, Laura Donaldson, Elizabeth Boardmore, Hubert Spekkens, Sharon Adams, and Gerry Dion. As well, I have been encouraged by the support of some very special colleagues: Frank Gavin, Ruth Colombo, Dennis Johnson, and John L. Tobias.

The book also benefited from the suggestions of colleagues who have used material from the unpublished manuscript in their classes — among them John Evans, Bob Mills, Jean Dawe, and Dale Anderson at Red Deer College and Dan Ryan, David McCarthy, and Kathy Hanford at Centennial College. For their many helpful comments on the manuscript, I would also like to thank my reviewers, Rosalind Robertson of St. Lawrence College, Bruce Hunter of Seneca College, and Robert C. Scott of Humber College. I am especially grateful to Jim MacDonald, also of Humber College, who read my manuscript with such care and made so many helpful suggestions. The book is better for all their input.

I owe a debt to Patrick Ferrier at Prentice-Hall, who saw promise in the original version despite its flaws; his commitment and positive outlook have cheered me greatly. I would like to thank Sandy Magico for her initial encouragement, and David Stover for his friendly support throughout the project.

I would like to acknowledge the contributions of my editors at Prentice-Hall: Monica Schwalbe, Jean Ferrier (MacDonald), and especially Maryrose O'Neill, whose keen attention to detail and good advice have won my eternal respect and gratitude.

As always, I have been assisted and encouraged in numberless ways, large and small, by Tim Turner. Without his enthusiasm and his belief in my work this task and others like it would have been unmanageable. This book is for him.

Effective Business Writing

CHAPTER 1

Style in Business Writing: An Overview

No skill is so vital to the practice of business, or indeed to everyday life, as effective communication. We live in a busy crowded world, and interact with dozens, maybe even hundreds, of people daily. In business, much of the contact we have with others is through the things we write, and thus much of our success in business may depend on writing clearly. It's easy to see how important it is to write and to edit carefully, so that you say exactly what you mean and avoid misunderstandings that can cost time, money, or loss of face.

Achieving clarity in writing takes effort, but the good news is that with effort almost anyone can learn to write effective business communications. Experienced business communicators have mastered both style and content in their letters, memos, and reports, but their mastery began with the recognition that all good business writing is based on two main principles, and all business communications are made up of essentially the same parts.

In order to communicate effectively, you must first be able to clearly state your primary objective. You can't express your meaning clearly unless you know what it is before you begin to write. Secondly, you must have a clear idea of the audience you are writing to. What is the reader's interest in this information? What background does this person have? What will the reader need to know to make a decision?

Once you have a clear idea of these two essentials, you can begin to organize your business communication. All business writing can be said to contain the same parts:

1. The main message statement ("the main thing I want to tell you is that . . ."). In a report, this is referred to as the summary. In a letter or memo, this information appears in the "re" or subject line.

2. Any background information required for the reader. This is your introductory sentence or paragraph or the introduction section of your report.

3. The full development of the letter, memo, or report. This part is referred to as the discussion or body of the work, and provides any necessary details.

4. The closing sentence or paragraph or section, known as the conclusion. It should remind your reader once again of your main point, and should indicate any outcome you expect or intend. It may also suggest to the reader any appropriate action he or she should take in response to your communication.

Keep these parts in mind, and always use them as a guide when you are writing your business communications. After all, you want your message to be communicated, and as writer you must help your reader to understand. Using these guidelines can make your writing more effective and the writing process easier because you will have organized your thoughts before writing them down.

A business communication of any kind also should be arranged attractively on the page. This means the writer should create an effective balance between the printed or written material (print) and the blank areas of the page (known as white space), where no print appears. A page which is crowded with print from one edge to the other without visual breaks may intimidate the reader; generous margins, paragraphing, and standardized formats can help a reader get your message more easily and quickly, and can also help make a good initial impression.

Now let us look more closely at these two important aspects of business communication 1) identifying your main objective and 2) identifying your reader's needs, expectations, and background knowledge.

Step One: Identifying the Main Point

Before you begin writing, ask yourself why you are writing this letter, report, or memo. What do you want it to do? This awareness is equally important whether you are writing a letter, a memo, or a report. Since the business letter and the memo are the most frequently used forms of business communication, we will begin with them. Reports, of course, are more complex, and these are dealt with in Chapters Four and Five.

Memos and letters may address only one issue, or involve a number of related issues. They may be as short as one page or as long as two or three pages. Whatever their length or contents, however, one principle remains constant: if you are not clear about exactly what you want to say, you cannot say it well. It is also important to organize your writing with your most important purpose foremost. You cannot hope to make your business writing effective unless you know in advance exactly what you want it to do. Keep the following points in mind when writing a letter or memo.

Be Specific

Make sure you can identify exactly what you wish your reader to know, and what response you expect. Be specific. For instance, if you wish to order supplies, book a room, or return materials, identify this purpose immediately. Put it at the beginning of your communication, preferably in a subject or "re" line. Don't waste your reader's time; get to the point immediately. Putting your main point first will seem awkward at the beginning, since we have all been conditioned to write in a more or less chronological order, which often results in the main point coming last. However, you can—and should—discipline yourself to put it first. If you begin your rough draft with "The main thing I want to tell you is that . . . ," you will find it easier to focus on your main message. You can delete this clause in your final draft.

Know Your Purpose

Recognize the main purpose of your communication. Is your primary aim to inform, or to persuade your reader? This "tell or sell" focus must be clear in your mind as you begin to write because your letter or memo will differ accordingly. If you are primarily interested in informing your reader, you can state your facts clearly and simply. If, however, you want to convince your reader of a specific point of view, you will need to use more persuasive techniques in your writing. These are covered in Chapter Three.

Simplify Your Message

Try to keep your letters and memos as simple as possible: don't clutter them with irrelevant information. If you can, it is best to stick to one main topic, and include only what is necessary to the reader's understanding of your message. If you must deal with several topics in one letter or memo, be sure that each is dealt with fully before moving to the next issue. Cluster related information, and get to the point as quickly as possible.

Step Two: Identifying Your Reader

Since any business communication is really an attempt to convince your intended reader that your position is valid and your recommendations necessary, you must present the information in a manner most likely to convince that specific reader. You are more likely to accomplish this if you first clearly identify this reader according to three criteria.

Needs

Consider first the information that your reader needs to have in order to make a decision. What is the reader's interest in this subject? How much detail is needed? Leave out any information that is not immediately relevant to the reader, no matter how interesting it may seem from your point of view. If you are to communicate your point successfully, you must address the reader's needs.

Background Knowledge

Keep in mind your reader's level of expertise. If you are writing to someone who has no prior knowledge of your project, you will need to explain substantially more than you will if you are writing to someone who is well-acquainted with it. On the other hand, it is as inconsiderate to provide unnecessary detail to someone who knows a great deal about your project as it is to provide inadequate detail to someone who does not know very much about it.

Expectations

What you say, and how you say it, will be very much affected by what the reader has been expecting from your work. A reader who has been expecting a negative response will be relieved and delighted by good news, making your writing task easier, but a reader who has been anticipating positive results is likely to be disappointed, frustrated, or angry when those expectations are not met. If you ignore or overlook your reader's frustrated expectations you will only aggravate the situation and you may damage your business relationship. On the other hand, acknowledging the reader's legitimate disappointment can help to cushion the impact of bad news and emphasize your professional concern and interest in the reader's viewpoint. Such positive reinforcement can go a long way toward cementing effective business relationships.

In order to make the communication a success, it is the writer's responsibility to identify the reader clearly so that the communication can be geared to the kind of reader who will receive the message.

Step Three: The Six C's of Business Writing

Beyond clearly identifying both your main message and your reader, you will also want to attend to the actual style of your writing. Good business writing—like any other effective writing—exhibits a number of identifiable characteristics.

1. Conciseness

Say as much as you need to say in as little space as possible without being curt. Leave out irrelevant details and avoid repeating yourself. Ask yourself whether the reader really needs to know a fact before you include it. Avoid wordy expressions and clichés, such as:

at this point in time	if this proves to be the case
it is probable that	it has come to my attention that
until such time as	please do not hesitate to

These are only a few; some others are provided in the following chapter. In any case, you should learn to recognize these deadeners of style and clarity, and eliminate them from your writing.

2. Clarity

This can be achieved by close attention to organization and specific detail. Be as concrete and specific as you can, identifying exactly what the problem is and what you would like done. Try to avoid ambiguous phrasing also: the message should be clear on the first brief reading. Your reader should never have to puzzle out your meaning, and should have no unanswered questions after reading your correspondence.

3. Cohesiveness

Any business correspondence should "hold together"; the parts should be logically connected one to the other, and you should use connectives to guide your reader from one point to the next. If you have organized your ideas well, cohesiveness should be easy to attain by the addition of connectives. Some that you may wish to use include:

since	as well as	in addition to
therefore	however	on the other hand
naturally	of course	as a matter of fact
also	nevertheless	for instance
for example	once again	furthermore
as a result	thus	

4. Correctness

Check the accuracy of all information—names, dates, places, receipt numbers, prices—that you include in a business communication. Correctness, of course, also includes correct spelling, grammar, and sentence structure. Never send a business letter without proofreading and correcting it first—to do so is extremely unprofessional, and a mistake could be costly. When you proofread you read with the clear intention of improving your written message; you look not only for errors in spelling and grammar, but also for any places where your message is unclear. If possible, take a break—even a short one—between the writing and the proofreading. The next chapter offers some more detailed advice on this important process.

5. Completeness

Make sure no important details have been overlooked. Have you included all of the information your reader will need in order to understand and act on your message? Always, after you've written a business letter, memo, or report, ask yourself "Have I said everything I needed to say?" Be sure you have answered any of these which are relevant:

Who?   What?   How many?
When?   Where?   How?
Why?

6. Courtesy

Be very careful of your tone in business communications; things usually go more smoothly if people are friendly to one another, and this is especially true in business. Always be pleasant, and be sure to say please and thank you for any services or favors requested or received. Even if you are writing to someone whom you believe has done you wrong, give this person the benefit of the doubt, at least initially: assume that the error was the unintentional result of a misunderstanding.

These Six C's are among the most important qualities of good business writing. If you can incorporate them into your own work, your writing will be vastly improved.

Of course, business communications depend on more than content for their effectiveness: the appearance of your letters also contributes to their success. An effective business letter or memo is typed with a clear, dark

Kayla Turner (1)
PO Box 123
Drayton Valley, Alberta
T5Y 7H8

9/28/89 (2)

Ministry of Tourism
Province of British Columbia
Parliament Buildings
Victoria, British Columbia

Dear Sir:

(3) I am writting (4) you this letter because (5) I am interested in taking a trip to British Columbia. It has come to my attention that (6) your ministry can offer some valueable (7) information to potential tourists who are concidering (8) visiting your beautiful province. (9)

It would be greatly appreciated (10) if you could provide me with some documents (11) outlining your attractions, accommodations, and special events.

Thank you in advance for your assistance in this matter (12). Your immediate response will be appreciated. (13)

Sincerly (14) yours,

Kayla Turner
Kayla Turner. (15)

Figure 1.1 *The first draft of Kayla Turner's letter of request contains many flaws. Try to identify the errors yourself before reading the analysis.*

ribbon on clean, good-quality paper. It makes use of generous margins, and never looks too crowded or too spaced out, and appears balanced on the page. It may make use of other visual effects to make it both attractive and easier to read. For example, if it includes several important facts, these may be indented in list form to set them apart from the rest of the information.

Figure 1.1 shows the first draft of a business letter which does not observe the Six C's or the rules of effective layout. Compare it carefully with the corrected version (Figure 1.2) noting where the improvements have been made and why. Errors in the first draft have been numbered for easy reference in the analysis.

A N A L Y S I S

1. Since her name appears under her signature, Kayla should not include it here.
2. She should write the date out in full for ease of understanding.
3. A subject line would help to clarify what Kayla seeks, and could replace the entire first paragraph.
4. Writing is misspelled.
5. "I am writing you this letter . . ." is clearly unnecessary: the reader, who has the letter in hand, does not need to be told that you have written it.
6. "It has come to my attention that . . ." is a cliché and should be avoided. It is also unnecessarily wordy and pompous.
7. Valuable is misspelled.
8. Considering is misspelled.
9. This kind of effusiveness borders on sickly sweet, and serves no useful purpose; Kayla should try to sound more genuine.
10. "It would be appreciated . . ." is not only a cliché, but it is passive voice.
11. The phrase "some documents" is vague: Kayla has not identified clearly what she wants. She needs to be specific about her needs.
12. "Thank you in advance for your attention to this matter" is another cliché, and it adds to the letter 's wordiness. A simple thank you will be enough.
13. "Your immediate response will be appreciated" is not only another unnecessarily wordy and tired phrase, but it borders on rudeness: Kayla implies that the people in the Ministry of Tourism won't respond quickly enough.
14. Sincerely is misspelled.
15. No period should follow her name.

PO Box 123
Drayton Valley, Alberta
T5Y 7H8

September 28, 1989

Ministry of Tourism
Province of British Columbia
Parliament Buildings
Victoria, British Columbia

Dear Sir or Madam:

Re: Tourism Information for Vancouver and area

I am planning a visit to British Columbia during Christmas
week and would appreciate any brochures or other information
you could provide regarding attractions, accommodations, and
special events in the Vancouver area from approximately
December 20, 1988 through January 3, 1989.

I plan to make the trip by car and expect to stay overnight
in the Kamloops area. I would also like some information
about accommodations in that area, if you have it, and would
appreciate a provincial road map as well.

I have heard many positive things about Vancouver, and am
looking forward to this trip. Thank you very much for
your help.

Sincerely,

Kayla Turner

Kayla Turner

Figure 1.2 *The improved version of Kayla's letter observes all of the Six C's of business writing.*

In addition to these mistakes, Kayla has made another major error in her first letter: she has not provided some of the specifics that would enable the people in the Tourism office to help her most effectively. She should indicate where in the province she plans to visit, and when she will be there. Activities and events vary around the province and are often seasonal.

As well, Kayla's letter is crowded too high up on the page, and no care has been taken to centre it vertically. Her margins could also be more generous, especially since her letter is so short. This kind of detail makes a letter more attractive and even more pleasant to read. Take a look at Kayla's improved letter (Figure 1.2).

A N A L Y S I S

1. Since Kayla does not know whether the reader of her letter will be male or female, she has observed courtesy by changing "Dear Sir" to "Dear Sir or Madam."
2. The subject or "re" line specifies what information she wants and for which area.
3. The opening paragraph avoids any clichés and gets right to the point: the request for information and the dates and destination of the planned visit.
4. Additional details about the trip help the reader to determine what information Kayla will need. She specifies some of the documents, such as a map, that she believes will be useful to her. Note that she includes her method of travel only because it affects what the ministry people will send her.
5. A brief compliment and her thanks close the letter effectively.

Note too that the layout of the letter has been improved: it has more generous margins and has been spaced more effectively so that it is not so crowded towards the top of the page.

THINGS TO TRY

Read the following business communications (Figures 1.3 and 1.4). Following the model analysis of Kayla Turner's letter, suggest ways they might be improved, keeping in mind all six principles of style in business writing.

Abbi Lawson
980 Main Street,
Saint John, New Brunswick
E1G 2M3

March 3, 1989

Mr. Toby Trapper, Director
Communications Corporation
555 California Street
Vancouver, British Street
V1R 7H9

Dear Sir:

I am writting you a letter to ask you about the book I ordered from
you about six weeks ago. I still haven't received it even though
you have already cashed my cheque. If you don't send it to me right
away I'll have to report you to the department of consumer affairs.

Yours truely,

Abbi Lawson

Abbi Lawson

Figure 1.3 *In how many ways does Abbi Lawson's letter violate the Six C's?*

```
                    MEMORANDUM

    To:   Mr. Astbury
          Department of English

    From: English 12A

    Date: September 30, 1989

    Re:   Problems with marking of last
    assignment

    We would like to get together with you to
    discuss the marks we received on the last
    assignment. Everybody in the class is
    upset with their grades and we don't think
    you explained clearly enough what you
    wanted anyway. We want to meet with you
    Thursday on your lunch hour to settle this
    problem. Please give us an answer in
    tomorrow's English class.


    Hilda Vander Zande
    Class Rep
```

Figure 1.4 *This memo is unlikely to help solve the problems the class has with Mr. Astbury. What is wrong here?*

CHAPTER 2

Sharpening Your Business Writing Style

It is one thing to grasp the theory of putting the main message first and weeding out wordy and clichéd phrases, but it's another entirely to actually do it. Most business writers experience difficulty in achieving the sharpness of style that they desire. It is easier to list the Six C's than it is to follow them! Conciseness and clarity seem to be the two most troublesome and, because they are closely linked, improving one often means improving the other. The only way to achieve clarity and conciseness is to increase organization and reduce wordiness. This process requires several drafts, but it can be learned, and you can use it to make your writing more effective.

Preparing to Write

Before you begin to write, plan your communication carefully. Using the Business Writing Planner (Figure 2.1) on the next page as a guide, identify the important elements of your message and the probable needs and expectations of your reader. Jot down the major points you wish to cover, and juggle them around to achieve the most logical order. Consider carefully the way in which these points can be presented, choosing your words with care as you work. Then write your rough draft, beginning with the phrase "The main thing I want to tell you is that . . ."

BUSINESS WRITING PLANNER

Before beginning your letter or memo, consider these points carefully.

1. What is the topic of this letter or memo?

2. What is my focus or purpose? Am I providing information or selling an idea?

3. What is my main point? (This will appear in a subject line.) "The main thing I want to say is that . . ."

4. Who is my reader? What is his or her interest in this subject? What does my reader already know and what further information will be needed or wanted?

5. What background information does my reader need as preparation for what I am going to say?

6. What are my primary supporting points? Which details are important? Have I answered any Who, What, Where, Why, and How questions the reader might have?

7. What, if any, action do I wish my reader to take after reading my letter or memo? Have I made it possible for her or him to do so?

Figure 2.1 *A business writing planner can help you in all your business communications.*

Common Faults of Business Writing

Once you have planned your letter or memo, you must look at it critically to determine whether it is as effective as it could be. Concise writing is hard work, and there is no one whose first drafts do not need correction. Although you should give some thought to planning and organization when you write the first draft, don't imagine that it will be perfect. Expect—and be willing—to revise your work to make it more effective. With practice, this process will become easier and less time-consuming. A good way to learn to edit your own writing is to look for specific, common faults of business writing. Here are some of the real troublemakers.

1. Failure to identify the central issue

Before you begin to write, be sure that you can identify your main idea and that you understand what you want your reader to know. This must come first, and it should be clearly expressed. Before you work on the body of the letter, write down your main idea. You may even, as we discussed, begin your rough draft with the words "The main thing I want to tell you is that . . . ." Cross out this clause for your final draft so that you begin with the main idea you wish to communicate. In fact, putting the point into a "re" line will not only force you to put it first, but will also help your reader to grasp your message more quickly.

2. Use of clichés

This is one of the most common faults in business writing, making it drab and uninteresting. Below are some of the most common clichés. There are others which should be avoided, but these will give you a taste of what to look for—as a general rule, any phrase which sounds as though it "ought" to be in a business letter probably should be eliminated from yours!

at this point in time	if this proves to be the case
in the amount of	it is probable that
postpone until later	under separate cover
it has come to my attention that	until such time as
reach a decision	on or before
please do not hesitate to	send you herewith
whether or not	with reference to
enclosed herewith find	at the present time
give consideration to	in view of the foregoing

due to the foregoing consideration	in accordance with your request
in the near future	it will be our earnest endeavor
at your earliest convenience	due to the fact that
in the event that	in accordance with your request

Inexperienced writers imagine that business writing is supposed to sound hackneyed, because that has been their experience as readers of business letters. Many business writers, not knowing what else to do, fall back on the clichés they have seen in the writing of others. Because such clichés add words without adding meaning or clarity, because they say in several words what could more clearly be said in one, and because they obscure rather than clarify your meaning, they are bad writing. Check your own writing for such phrases and replace them with more direct language.

3. Use of the passive voice

The passive voice expresses not action done by the subject, but action done to the subject, a crucial difference. For example, "Assistance would be greatly appreciated" is better written "I would appreciate your assistance . . . ." In certain types of very formal writing the use of passive voice is considered appropriate, but it distances writer from reader, deadens style, and often causes a loss of clarity. For example, consider how much more vivid and powerful, not to mention shorter, are the following sentences when they are written in active voice.

Larry completed my project.

is better than

The project which I was working on has been completed by Larry.

Shirley completed the required tests.

is better than

The tests which were required have been completed by Shirley.

We have evaluated your application.

is better than

Your application has been evaluated by us.

Doug hired John Smith to complete the Ferguson project.

is better than

John Smith was hired by Doug for the completion of the project for the Ferguson account.

One way you can make your own writing more powerful and concise is to eliminate unnecessary use of passive voice wherever you can.

4. Overuse of phrases and dependent clauses as modifiers

Very often we find ourselves using several words where we could use just one. Excessive use of phrasal and clausal modifiers is among the most common causes of wordiness. As a rule, you should not use several words when one will do the job. See how much more concise these examples can be:

— the project I am working on	— my project
— the equipment which our departmentrecently acquired	— our recently acquired equipment
— the store on the corner	— the corner store
— the present which I bought for my father	— my father's present, or even my present for my father
— the account belonging to this customer	— this customer's account
— the reason for which I am writing	— my reason for writing
— the business which I recently aquiried	— my recently acquired business
— property which belongs to the company	— company property
— a friend whom I have known for a long period of time	— a longtime friend

Watch, in particular, an overuse of the words *of* (or other prepositions), *which*, or *that*. Rewrite such phrases or clauses into one or two words whenever you can do so without a loss of precision or thought.

5. Repetition of ideas

In a memo or a letter, say what you mean in as few words as possible. To make your writing really effective, you should avoid any unnecessary repetition. To this problem, cluster related information and make each point only once. If you say it clearly the first time, you can eliminate the useless and often confusing repetition that weakens your writing and obscures your message.

6. Failure to cluster related points

In organizing your message, you must be sure to cluster your points appropriately: jumping back and forth is confusing to the reader. If, for example, you are writing a letter to obtain tickets and accommodations for a convention, you should put all information pertaining to the tickets into one paragraph, and all information about the accommodations into another. For added clarity and visual appeal, you can place the main details in indented lists.

7. Failure to identify the action desired

Often you will write letters requiring the reader to perform some kind of action. Although you may feel that the appropriate course of action is obvious, what you want done may not be quite so clear to the reader, whose idea of a suitable solution may differ from yours. Don't expect your reader to come to the same conclusion you have reached. State directly, in clear and specific language, what you expect the reader to do. If there are several steps to be taken, list and enumerate them for the reader's convenience.

8. Incomplete information

Before writing your final draft, check once more to be sure you have included all relevant information. Ask yourself Who? What? Where? When? Why? and How?, to be sure that you have supplied all the necessary details.

POINTS TO REMEMBER

Learning to edit out these weaknesses will improve your writing and make your messages easier to understand and act upon. Keep these rules in mind whenever you write a piece of business communication. Here they are in summary, with a few additions:

1. Be prepared to write more than one draft.
2. Always begin with your main idea.
3. Put this information into a subject line where possible.
4. Cluster related points together.
5. Check wordiness by eliminating unnecessary repetition, excessive use of clauses and phrases, clichés, and the passive voice.

6. Include all necessary information.
7. Identify desired action.
8. Be courteous—watch your tone.

THINGS TO TRY

SECTION A

Revise the following sentences, taken from business communications, to make them clearer and more concise.

1. In the event that any employee should be the final individual to exit the premises of this company on the eve of any given working period, it would be greatly appreciated by management as a gesture of fiscal responsibility if such individuals should leave the offices in a state of darkness.

2. It has come to my attention that your firm is offering a new position that has never been available before to any new applicants from outside the company. Please be advised that I would like to express my interest in this very attractive position and feel that you should be interested in my background as well.

3. If this writer can be of any further assistance to you in this matter, please do not hesitate to contact myself at the above-mentioned office location.

4. With reference to your communication of the above-referenced date, enclosed herewith find the documents which you requested at that point in time.

5. At the present time, I am not at liberty to give consideration to such requests due to the inability of this office to evaluate whether or not this aforementioned request is in accordance with present practice of this company.

6. It is our earnest endeavor to process applications with greatest efficiency; however, in the event that you are not in receipt of a requested response on or before the closing date, please do not hesitate to put yourself in contact with personnel at this location.

7. Due to the difficulties involved with the aforementioned request, I

would like to take this opportunity to thank you in advance for your assistance in this difficult matter.

8. Due to the fact that this writer was unavailable over the period of the previous month because of absence due to vacation, your correspondence of the above-referenced date did not receive the immediate attention of myself, for which I send you herewith my most sincere apology.

9. A cheque for the amount specified to cover the loss experienced due to the above incident of April 30 has been prepared by this office. You appearance is requested at your earliest convenience to complete the necessary paperwork and to receive such payment. We trust this is in order.

10. In the event of circumstances beyond our control which affect delivery of this service, some alterations to the planned schedule may be required.

SECTION B

The following business communications are real examples which I have collected over several years (Figures 2.2 to 2.5). Read them through to spot weaknesses similar to those we've discussed above, and edit for conciseness and clarity.

IGA Groceteria
25 Headframe Street
Forestville, Ontario
K8Y 4R2

April 25, 1989

Dr. Donald Dinero, Pharmacist
Value Drugs
34 Centre Street
Cedarville, Ontario
K7Y 2F6

Dear Dr. Dinero:

With reference to your correspondence dated April 22, 1989, in accordance with your request for information about Patrick Hare, it will be my most earnest endeavor to provide you with a most glowing reference of his character.

First of all, Patrick Hare was in our employ for a period of four years; he is at the present time seeking for a position in a more advanced capacity elsewhere. During that period of time Patrick performed a wide variety of duties which were expected of him in his position of stock person and clerk which he performed to the utmost of his ability. We never had at any time a reason to doubt Patrick's ability to be able to do his job and we perceived at all times that he was a good worker who was conscientious in his work, honest, and utilized courtesy in dealings with customers.

In giving consideration to Patrick's personal characteristics of his personality, in line with your suggestion, we have found Patrick to be easy to get along with for everybody who had to work with him and at all times could be depended upon to do what was needed at that point.

Due to the foregoing considerations, it would make me happy to be able to provide you herewith with a positive recommendation of Patrick and in the event the you are in need of further information, please do not hesitate to contact myself in the near future.

Yours very sincerely,

Frank Bilborson
Manager

Figure 2.2 *Despite his good intentions, Frank Bilborson's message is obscured by wordy, vague writing. See if you can improve his letter.*

September 26, 1989

Jennifer MacLennan
5419 39 Street
Red Deer AB T4N 1A1

Re: Policy# CH-BINDER (AUTO 83 HONDA CIVIC WGN)
       Effective September 16, 1988 to March 16, 1989

Dear Jennifer:

Please be advised that Canadian Home has written us
requesting a copy of your drivers license (front and
back). This is because the number we submitted was
rejected by Motor Vehicles.

Kindly send this to our office as soon as possible. Your
immediate attention to this matter would be appreciated.
We thank you in advance for your cooperation.

Trusting this is in order.

Sincerely yours,
LEARNERS INSURANCE LTD.

Leola Burdett

Leola Burdett
B/pe

Figure 2.3   *Why might I have trouble responding to this request? What flaws can you find in this letter?*

CAREER STATEMENT: WHY I CHOSE EARLY CHILDHOOD DEVELOPMENT

When interacting with people, I find it most intriguing working with preschool children in this particular field, Early Childhood Development gives you a better in-depth look at what certain behaviors and ideas affect the different stages of development in young children.

Communication is the most important part of Early Childhood Development. Communicating with the children, their parents, as well as their teachers gives you an opportunity to observe human nature. Observing human nature with children is a very good example of getting to know the child.

When observing human nature, you find the different aspects of children, such as What are the child's likes and dislikes? How artistic/creative are they? What are the child's reactions to ideas?

These are just some of the eexamples and questions you will be asking when you begin to observe children.

By getting to know children as you work with them you will feel good and better about yourself when you look back on those special moments that you will always treasure.

As I look back at all the experience which I received when taking care of children. I found the observations which I did, to be very challenging, interesting, and very useful for comparisons.

Figure 2.4 *This career statement fails to deliver a clear, coherent message. How would you improve it?*

During the beginning of last year's school year, I tutored students between grades 2-3 level with arithmetic and phonics. For each evening with them. I tried to think of new ways to explain a problem which they found difficult. After each tutoring session I would record each observation about each child.

By the end of the school year, their was a tremendous change of each which I tutored. The children, their parents, as well as the teachers were quite amazed. I received a great many thanks and appreciation notes for the time that I spent with them. I felt good about myself and for the time I spent with them. It was challenging and very rewarding to be with them.

Figure 2.4 *(Continued)*

Lucy Peabody
27 Wormsley Road
Airdrie, Alberta
T4X 1U7

November 25, 1989

Contemporary Fashions
Manager, Nancy Schindelhauer
1702 Trutch Street
Vancouver, British Columbia
V8K 8H9

Dear Ms. Schindelhauer:

I am writing to tell you about my new pink sweater which
I bought from your catalogue last summer. I have always
liked your service in your store and enjoy dealing with
you. I am returning the sweater to you.

Your catalogues are always nice and clear and the
pictures are beautiful, which is what led me to order
this one from you in your Spring and Summer catalogue, on
page 26.

I am really writing because the one I got was size 16 and
I ordered size 12 in August I think. I need the right one
sent back right away because I am planning to wear it
over my Christmas holidays. It was $29.95.

Thank you very much for your help in fixing this mistake.
If you can't send it to me would you please refund my
money I paid you?

Yours sincerely,

Lucy Peabody

PS The sweater is catalogue number 307 - 62WP

Figure 2.5 *Though Lucy has included most of the necessary details, her letter is ineffective. Why?*

CHAPTER 3

Business Letters and Memos

Whether they are sent by surface mail, by facsimile machine, or through computer transmission, the business letter and the memo are the most common forms of business communication. Whenever someone in a company exchanges written information with someone in another firm, the business letter provides the appropriate vehicle. Within the company too, communication may take a written form called a memorandum. Although information can be exchanged by telephone, this method isn't satisfactory for all situations. For many practical reasons, written communication may be preferred: it allows a precision not possible in oral exchanges, and creates a permanent record for your own files. If a message must be sent across the country, the mail is still much cheaper than long distance telephone calls.

Generally, you should use a written form for your communication whenever

- You are sending the same information to several people
- A copy of the information you are sending must be retained on file
- The information concerns organization policy
- The document is to be distributed by carbon or photocopy to someone other than the individual to whom it is addressed

You should use a letter or a memo rather than a telephone call for any information which might be considered "official"; a call or even a personal note will suffice if the information is for one person only, no copies will be distributed elsewhere, and it is not for the record.

Because business letters and memos are used so frequently, consistent standards of content, format, and style have evolved to help make the task of writing easier. Meeting these standards in your writing will not only help to make your message more easily understood, but will also create a professional impression. Both memos and letters observe the same rule: get to the point and don't waste the reader's time. To be effective, they must be professional: accurate, clear, and written in an acceptable format.

Business letters and memos can carry both good news and bad, and may serve a multitude of purposes, from providing information to selling merchandise. Whatever their purpose, all business letters and memos can be divided into two main categories: request and response. Though the information below is specifically addressed to letters, memos follow the same general guidelines.

A **letter of request** may be written for any number of purposes: to order merchandise; to request information (printed materials, catalogues, travel fliers) or an appointment; to reserve a conference or hotel room; to apply for a job; to ask for favours (a reference, for instance); to sell merchandise.

Basically, a letter of request is any letter that initiates contact with another person, and establishes an effective working relationship between correspondents.

Request letters should observe the Six C's listed in Chapter One, keeping in mind that courtesy also means making reasonable requests—don't ask the person to whom you are writing to do your work for you. Here are three questions to ask yourself before you write:

1. Am I being specific about what I want to know or what I'd like done?
2. Am I asking someone else to find information or perform a task that I could easily accomplish myself?
3. Is this request going to inconvenience the person in any unreasonable way?

If you can easily find out the information you need from a library or other source, or if you are vague about exactly what you want, you should reconsider your request carefully. Of course, you should be sure to say please and thank you.

A **letter of response** is any letter written in response to a request, an advertisement, or a situation. These might include letters of recommendation, information, congratulations or condolence, or adjustment or complaint.

Once again, the Six C's apply, with a few additions. In a letter of response, you should be prompt, as well as helpful. Always give the reader a positive impression, and make your letter complete.

Good News and Bad News Messages

Within the two general categories of request and response, there are many situations which may require business letters and memos. These sometimes difficult situations may require either "good news" or "bad news" letters or memos, written for purposes of congratulations, complaint, sales, or refusals. Some of these present special problems for a beginning writer. Though business letters and memos carrying good news make it easy to establish a positive writer-reader relationship, those that carry bad news—letters of complaint or refusal, for example—are unlikely to please the reader.

In such letters, it is especially important to watch your tone. Try to cushion your bad news message with positive language. Be especially careful to avoid suggesting or implying that the other person is somehow responsible for the situation, even if you believe this to be the case. What you really want is to have the problem solved, and creating unnecessary bad feelings will only lessen the chances of this happening. Be pleasant and especially careful to avoid sarcasm.

All of these messages require the same qualities of conciseness, cohesiveness, correctness, and completeness as other business correspondence. They also contain an especial emphasis on courtesy. In a difficult or challenging situation, especially one in which bad news is being presented, it is particularly important to be courteous to your correspondents in order to make certain that your wishes are complied with.

1. *Congratulations or Acknowledgement*

Of the four special types, this good news letter is the most pleasant to write. A letter (or memo) of congratulations may be written to an employee, a colleague, or a client on the occasion of an achievement or accomplishment. This accomplishment may be an award, the publication of a book or article, a promotion, a significant contribution to a company project, or simply recognition of long and/or effective service. Whatever the occasion, the letter of acknowledgement/congratulations should be positive in tone and to-the-point. Such letters should be

- Specific (Identify the achievement/occasion)
- Positive (Make sure your tone is warm and your comments flattering)
- Sincere (Nothing is more insulting than congratulations which do not sound sincere. Avoid being too effusive.)
- Brief (As in any business communication, say what you have to say, then stop. Many people ruin effective acknowledgement or congratulations messages by not knowing when to quit.)

COMMUNICATIONS CORPORATION

INTERDEPARTMENTAL COMMUNICATION

DATE: April 14, 1990

TO: Gwynne Logan

FROM: Michael Cea

Re: Appreciation of your contributions during the
      1989/90 Fiscal year

Just a note to say thank you for all the work you have
done for the Publishing Division during this past year. I
have especially appreciated your willingness to aid in the
vacation period when I needed someone to fill in for ill
personnel, and to take on an extra book publishing project
when one of our other editors left the company.
Considering that you also managed to design a new training
program for the Staff Development Department, your
contribution has been truly commendable and beyond any
requirements of your job description.

Thank you for all that you have done and for your valuable
assistance. Few, if any, members of the division have
done more to make this a successful year. Please accept
my heartfelt thanks for a job well done.

Michael Cea

cc.   Personnel File
      Toby Trapper

MC:jm

Figure 3.1 *Note how Michael Cea's warm tone and use of specific details make his letter of congratulations effective?*

Figure 3.1 contains a memo of acknowledgement from a supervisor to a staff member who has contributed an extraordinary year's work to the company.

2. *Complaint*

Though not so pleasant to write, these bad news messages are unfortunately much more common than letters of congratulation. Although most businesses do their best to handle orders, requests, and other correspondence in a professional and efficient manner, occasionally mix-ups do occur. Orders may be misplaced, cheques lost, wrong merchandise sent, or mailings waylaid. Most firms will do all in their power to keep such mistakes from happening, since businesses function more smoothly when good will is maintained by effective customer relations. If you make it a rule to always assume that the mix-up is an honest error and to treat such incidents as unintentional, your complaints will be dealt with more promptly and positively.

The first rule for letters or memos of complaint is to be especially courteous. No one wants to receive abusive, sarcastic, or threatening letters; phrase your bad news in as positive terms as possible. Problems will be more easily smoothed out if you allow your correspondents room to correct the situation without making them look foolish. They will be more interested in helping you and they will be more anxious to maintain your good will if you approach them in a friendly, non-threatening manner.

It is also important that in a complaint you specifically identify the nature of the problem and the action you wish taken. For example, if you have ordered merchandise and after waiting a reasonable length of time have not received your order, you will want to identify the missing items by name, catalogue or item number, color and size (if applicable), catalogue issue, and page. You should state the date of your order, the cheque number if there is one, and the amount of the order. If you have a standing account with the firm, cite your account number. Be sure that all of this information is correct. Be sure also that you tell the reader exactly what you want done about the problem. The reader's idea of a satisfactory solution may differ from yours.

Here, then, are the points to remember for letters of complaint:

- Phrase your comments positively.
- Be sure to identify the exact nature of the problem immediately.
- Provide all relevant details.
- Request specific action.
- Be courteous. Thank correspondents for their help.

90 Victoria Crescent
Scarborough, Ontario
M2E 2R4

November 20, 1989

Accounting and Process Control
National Exchange Bank Student Loan Business
PO Box 12345
Rochester, New York
10098

Re: Returned cheques dated November 1, 1989 and December 1,
       1989
       Loan Payment Account #555693737 - 9

I received the above cheques from you, with a letter indicating
that they were rejected by my bank due to insufficient funds.
However, the cheques were processed by your department on
October 20, 1989 and received by my bank on October 25. The
reason for their rejection was thus not insufficient funds but
postdating. Although American banks may operate differently,
Canadian banks do not accept postdated cheques.

I dated the cheques according to their payment dates, and
mailed them in advance to make certain that they would reach
you on time. Since I would like to prevent such a mix-up
happening again, is there some way to ensure that in future my
cheques are not processed until the appropriate dates have
arrived?

I am enclosing a third cheque to cover both payments. Since
the original cheques reached you before the November 1 and
December 1 due dates, I would appreciate an adjustment to any
additional interest charges. Thank you.

Sincerely,

Craig Steele

Figure 3.2   *Even though the loans officer is at fault, Craig Steele is careful to maintain a positive tone. He will be more likely to win the assistance of his reader because he avoids anger and sarcasm.*

In Figure 3.2 Craig Steele is making a complaint regarding some student loan payment cheques that have been mistakenly processed too early, and have been rejected by his own bank. Note that though the loans officer is at fault, Craig wisely does not cause more difficulty by being sarcastic or abusive.

3. Sales or Persuasive Messages

Throughout this book, I have emphasized the necessity in any business writing of identifying the reader's needs, expectations, and interests. Such an understanding of your reader is necessary if you are to write effective business communications, but is especially crucial when you move from merely informative to persuasive writing. Sales letters are the most common form of persuasive writing. Though these can be considered good news letters, and should, like the previous types, be very positive in tone, they are a bit more challenging to write. You want to appeal to your readers, influencing them either to purchase your product or service, or to provide some authorization or funding. You must sound upbeat and personal, and above all, sincere. Outline to the reader the advantages of the item(s) you are offering. Keep your letter personal; don't bully, patronize, or pander to the reader.

Sales letters may be sent to potential customers, or to established clients of your firm; your approach will differ slightly depending on which is the case for you. Here are some of the things your sales letter to a new customer should do:

• Catch the reader's attention immediately. You may do this with a question, an unusual statement, a story, or a quotation, or you may offer a premium or gift for prompt responses.
• Create a desire for the product you're offering. Show your readers the advantages of buying your product. If it will save time, work, or money, show how this will be accomplished.
• Make it easy for the reader to acquire the product. Provide an order form, a postage-paid envelope, or instructions as to how to place an order by phone. Offer installment payments.
• Keep an enthusiastic tone. If you can, use the reader's name to make the message more personal.
• Be sure to sound sincere, as a natural extension of being sincere. If you don't sound as though you mean what you say, your reader will reject your message, no matter how earnest you feel. Be sure that your sincerity is reflected in what you write.

The sales letter to an established client is nearly identical, with a few additions:

- As an established client, your reader will be more predisposed to read your mailer through, so you do not have to work quite so hard to catch attention.
- The established client has already shown interest in the products you're offering. Briefly emphasize the advantages of your products, and outline any improvements or new lines.
- Make it easy for the client to acquire the product.
- Be enthusiastic. Here you should definitely use the reader's name to personalize your letter.
- Be sincere, and emphasize the effective relationship you've had in the past.

All sales letters must appeal to the reader strongly enough to make that person respond actively. They should be positive, warm, and persuasive, appealing to the needs, interests, and expectations of the reader.

A Note on the "Hard Sell"

Sales writing, as a form of persuasive writing, requires careful identification of reader needs. This is a perfectly legitimate, basic principle of promotional literature, and in fact underlies all effective business communication. However, there are other bases of appeal that are less respectable: instead of identifying and responding to an existing need, some promotional material seeks to create a need for a product. This kind of advertising appears to be designed to manipulate readers by appealing to their greed or to their fears and doubts instead of to their needs. Some sales fliers use an hysterically enthusiastic style and tone. Many modern readers are becoming wary of this hard sell approach, and may be turned off by it. Remember to keep your tone positive and warm, not loud and offensive.

The following memo (Figure 3.3) encourages personnel in a placement agency to take advantage of the company's Referral Bonus Program by recruiting experienced help.

4. *Refusals*

These bad news messages are often the most difficult to write. Great delicacy is required whenever you have to turn down someone's request, whether that request has come from a candidate for employment or from a client who wants an adjustment for a used or damaged product.

Here, as in all bad news letters or memos, tone is important. You wish to

TEMP-PRO

The best help when you need it most!

TO: All Temporary Employees

FROM: Mary Morgan, Placement Coordinator

DATE: November 18, 1990

RE: Temp-Pro's Referral Bonus Program

Did you know that you could earn cash for every qualified person you send to us? Our Referral Bonus Program pays you $50 for each qualified friend you refer!

Because of our recent growth, we have a real shortage of competent temporary employees for a variety of assignments. Do you know anyone who might be interested in working temp? Maybe someone you know is new to the city, or has recently left a job; perhaps you know students who are tired of being given the run-around by their service. You can do a friend—and us—a favour, and at the same time do something for yourself, when you invite someone you know to take advantage of the excellent placements offered by Temp-Pro Services.

You have reason to be proud of our record: Temp-Pro's reputation is built on service, to our customers and to our temporaries. We never forget that our temps—you—have helped to make us the largest and most dedicated company in the industry. And because you make our business the success it is, I want to do my best for you.

A brochure describing the Referral Bonus Program is attached, or you can find out more about it by phoning me at 555 6789 or dropping by the office to chat. I look forward to seeing you and your friends soon!

Figure 3.3 *The positive tone, the use of incentive, and the personal touch make Mary Morgan's promotional memo effective.*

be tactful in refusing to provide the service, and you wish to preserve the client's good will if possible. You must observe the rule of putting the main message first, but you should use as positive terms as possible to cushion the refusal, and especially avoid sarcasm or accusation. State the message briefly, and then explain your reasons politely.

It is important in refusal letters to accept responsibility for your decision, even if you feel that the person you are writing to is in some way at fault. Always stress your own inability to comply with the request. For example, if you are writing a letter of refusal to someone who has been turned down for a job, stress that the position was offered to another candidate because that individual more closely suited your needs, not because the person you are writing to is inadequate. Likewise, if you are refusing a reference, it is better to stress your inability to supply it, rather than suggest that the person is flawed. Here are some points to keep in mind when writing a letter of refusal:

- Identify the subject in a subject or re line.
- Indicate briefly your inability to comply with the reader's request, using as positive terms as possible.
- State your reasons simply, taking responsibility for your refusal.
- Avoid sarcasm or accusation.
- Be polite and sincere.
- Suggest someone else your correspondent might approach for assistance, if possible.
- Offer the person your best wishes for better success elsewhere if it's appropriate.

In the letter of refusal in Figure 3.4, the bad news has been cushioned with positive comments, and the reader has been invited to submit future work to the magazine. As well, the writer has recommended another publication that might accept the submission.

Remember, no matter what kind of letter or memo you are writing, you will want to be sure to identify your main point first, and communicate your message as clearly and concisely as possible, maintaining a polite tone throughout.

The Parts of a Business Letter

Whatever their purpose, all business letters contain the same parts and may be written in any of three standard formats. All are also single-spaced. Before we look at formats, let's consider the parts of a standard business letter.

Great Canadian Outdoors

The magazine for those with a zest for living!

February 15, 1989

Mr. Tom Roberts
55 Elwood Close
Calgary, Alberta
T5W 3F6

Dear Mr. Roberts

Thank you for submitting the article on your wilderness trek
through the Northwest Territories.

Though the subject matter is interesting and the accompanying
pictures attractive, I am afraid that we will not be able to
publish your article. Unfortunately, the approach you have
taken does not quite coincide with our editorial focus, which
is less adventure-oriented than this article.

I would like to encourage you in finding a publisher for your
work. You might try submitting it to Martin Veblin at Great
Northern Adventure. I believe that, with some revision yours
might be the sort of material that they use.

However, before submitting the article again, you really should
consider some close editing. A well-written article that
doesn't require polishing by the magazine is more likely to
find favor with a busy editorial staff.

Despite our inability to use the article, we would like to
extend our best wishes in placing this article with another
magazine.

Sincerely

Tim D. Turner
Managing Editor

90 Dalhousie Street, Edmonton, Alberta T5Y 3R7
(403) 987 0921   TELEX 22-7854

Figure 3.4 *Even though Tom Roberts' article has been rejected, he will appreciate Tim Turner's encouragement and recommendation of alternatives.*

1. **Return Address**   This is the normal address of the writer of the letter; it does not include the writer's name. In a personal business letter, the return address is your home address; if you are writing on behalf of your company, it is the company's name and address. If your company has a letterhead form (most do), you should use it for business correspondence and dispense with the return address.

2. **Date**   Though there is a move toward dating letters numerically, most of the time it is better to write the date out; there is as yet little consistency in the style of numerical dating, and this lack can cause confusion. There are currently three forms in use:

Canadian	27/06/89	Day/Month/Year
American	06/27/89	Month/Day/Year
"Metric"	89/06/27	Year/Month/Day

If your particular employer uses numerical dating, you should do so too, but otherwise, write the date out in full.

3. **Inside Address**   This is an important part of the business letter; it provides information for the files of the company to which it is sent. It should include the following, in this order:

Mr. Toby Trapper, Director	Name and title
Communications Corporation	Name of company/organization
555 California Street	Address of company
Vancouver, British Columbia	
V1R 7H9	

If the person's title is very long, it might be placed on a separate line, but the order of the parts remains the same:

Ms. Soo Liang Chan	Name
Assistant Manager of Human	Title
Resources	
Communications Corporation	Name of company/organization
555 California Street	Address of company
Vancouver, British Columbia	
V1R 7H9	

4. **Salutation**   This is the opening of your letter; traditionally, it's "Dear . . . ." Use the name of the person to whom you are writing, if you know it. If you don't know it, and it is important that you have it, (for instance, in a job application letter), telephone the company and ask the person's name. If you can't bring yourself to do this, you may wish to delete the salutation

altogether. In modern correspondence, this is permissible. It's not advisable to use "Dear Sir" if you don't know the name of the person to whom you're writing, since women now occupy many positions of authority and might object to the assumption that all such positions are held by men.

If you are corresponding with a person whose given name is not readily identifiable as male or female—for example, T.D. Turner, Terry Ferguson, Raj Bhanot, Saran Narang, or Mai Li Chiu—you may wish to write the full name in the salutation: "Dear T.D. Turner" or "Dear Mai Li Chiu." Unless you are on very friendly terms with the person you are writing to, note that it is never proper to use a first name. "Dear Terry" or "Dear Mai Li" is unacceptable.

5. **Subject or "Re" Line** This useful device is borrowed from the memorandum. It has become an important part of the business letter, since it forces the writer to observe the rule of putting the main information first, and allows the reader to identify the main point immediately. This line should be brief and to-the-point: it should indicate clearly what the letter is about. It will usually consist of a single phrase or two.

6. **Body** This contains the main information you wish to communicate, in as clear a form as possible. Identify the subject matter at the beginning, giving a brief outline of the situation or problem. Follow this with some pertinent details, carefully selected and organized so that the reader may easily understand your message. Finish with a specific statement which outlines what you expect of the reader. The body of the letter is single spaced, and divided into brief paragraphs for ease of reading. The number of paragraphs can vary depending on the complexity of the subject matter, as can the length of the letter. Some letters are two or three pages long, but most are one page. Whatever the length of the letter, its message should be easily grasped in one reading. If your reader must reread the letter several times simply to understand it, it is poorly composed and ineffective.

7. **Complimentary Closing** This can be any one of a variety of forms; the most common nowadays is "Sincerely " or even "Yours sincerely." "Yours truly" is not used very much anymore, though it isn't wrong. Whichever you use, be sure to note its correct spelling. If you are on very friendly terms with your correspondent, you may even wish to use a more familiar closing, such as "Cordially" or "Best wishes." Do not use these for more formal correspondence, however. If you are in doubt, simply use "Sincerely."

8. **Company Name** Occasionally, a writer using company letterhead will signify that correspondence is written on behalf of his or her employer by placing the company name, in block letters, immediately below the complimentary closing, above the writer's signature. This precaution is observed

to clarify responsibility for legal purposes. In the past, anything written on the company's letterhead was assumed to be on behalf of the firm, but frequent use of letterhead for personal correspondence has made this assumption impractical. Modern writers may take this extra measure to emphasize that the contents of the letter are indeed a matter of company business. It is not necessary to include this line in your business letters, but if it is common practice in your company, by all means do it.

Yours sincerely,
COMMUNICATIONS CORPORATION

Toby Trapper

Toby Trapper

9. **Signature**   This is the name of the writer only; it should not include any nicknames, titles, or degrees. A business person also uses a consistent signature, not Jennifer in one letter and Jen or Jenny in the next. Choose one form of your name (preferably not a diminutive) and use it consistently.

10. **Typed Name and Titles**   Since many signatures are unreadable, a courteous writer includes the typed name beneath the signature. If you wish to include any degrees or titles, do that here. (These are not, you will remember, included with the signature.) If your name is one of those which do not indicate gender, you may wish to indicate a choice of title. This could make it easier for your correspondent to reply to you. Very often you will also wish to include your position in the organization you represent.

Terry Lansdown (Mrs.) Chief of Operations	A.J. Smith (Dr.) Chief of Staff
Soo Liang Chan (Ms.) Assistant Manager of Human Resources	Saran Narang (PhD) Editor in Chief

11. **Secretary's Notations**   These are used again for record purposes; it is sometimes important to know who typed the correspondence, whether any enclosures or attachments were included, and/or whether any other people received carbon copies or photocopies. The notations appear in the lower left of the page, and are as follows:

/jml   Secretary's initials; some organizations use this form to indicate that the secretary actually composed the correspondence on behalf of the writer, though this is not the case in every firm

TT/jml	Writer's initials/typist's initials; may be written this way to indicate that the secretary typed what was written by someone else
encl: 2	Enclosure notation—indicates that two items were enclosed with the package
attach: 3	Attachment notation—similar to enclosure notation, but items were appended to letter with a clip or staple. In this instance, there were three.
cc. T. Turner B. Halloran	These people received carbon or photocopies of the correspondence. Though 'cc' is commonly used, this notation might also appear as 'pc' for photocopy. In either case, its meaning is the same.

12. **File Number** A code consisting of a combination of letters and numbers may appear at the lower left or, more commonly, at the upper right of the page; this is a file number which assists the business in filing correspondence in the appropriate location.

The Parts of a Memo

Although the letter and memo serve similar purposes and may carry similar kinds of messages, a memo is intended to remain inside the company or institution, and this affects its structure. It has no need of an inside address, return address, or salutation; instead it has a relatively standard heading made up of four parts. The labels To, From, Date, and Re (or Subject) are usually arranged vertically at the top left-hand side of the memo. The other sections of the memo are similar to the parts of the business letter, as explained below.

1. To   Takes the place of the salutation and identifies, by name and title, the person or persons to whom the memo is directed.

2. From   Identifies, again by name and title, the person who wrote the memo.

3. Date   On which the memo was written; you may wish to use numerical dating style in a memo, but as we discussed above, numerical dating can cause confusion, and you should probably avoid it unless your firm recommends it.

4. Re or Subject   Identifies for the reader exactly what issue the memo addresses, and what you wish to say about that issue. This most crucial line of your memo should contain the main point you have identified in your rough draft with the key words "The main thing I want to tell you is that . . . " Business people are busy, and will not want to scan the entire memo to find the gist of it. Often they decide whether or not to take the time to read the memo by glancing at the subject line, so make sure yours is specific.

5. Message   The body of the memo, without a salutation, follows the headings. It may be separated from them by a solid line if you wish. Like the body of the letter, it contains the main information you wish to communicate, in as clear a form as possible. It is single spaced, and deals with the situation or problem as specifically as possible.

Like a business letter, a memo may deal with issues of varying complexity. Memos used for simple issues are usually less than a page long, but the memo format may also be used for a short report dealing with more complex situations. Whatever its purpose, the memo, like the business letter and report, provides specifics to support the main point given in the subject or re line. However, because it is often very short and to the point, a memo risks being curt or abrupt in tone. You will want to be especially careful to observe courtesy in a memo, in order to avoid offending your reader.

As well, you should avoid contributing to the flurry of unnecessary memos. Use a memo only for information which might be considered "official"; a casual message may better be delivered by telephone or by a brief personal note.

6. Initial or Signature   No complimentary closing is required on a memo, but it may be initialed or signed if you wish. Though a signature is not absolutely necessary, it is becoming more common to sign memos. Since your name appears at the top, there is no need to type it again under your signature.

7. Notations   Since memos serve the same purposes as letters, they make use of the same notations, especially secretary's initials and carbon copy designations. If it is appropriate, copies may be sent to superiors or other interested parties within the company. For example, a supervisor who writes a memo commending an employee for work well done might direct a copy to the personnel file; the head of a departmental committee might direct a copy of a meeting announcement to the department head to let that individual know that the committee is getting on with its work. Memos, like business letters, may also contain file numbers for easy reference.

Letter and Memo Format

Business letters may employ one of three formats widely used in Canada: semiblock, full block, and modified semiblock. The semiblock style is the oldest pattern and although it is still widely used, it is gradually being replaced by the full block style. Modified semiblock is a transitional form, a blending of the other two styles. Memos, with clear cut headings at the top of the page, have a simpler format than letters and so are generally easier to construct.

Whichever letter format you use, you should give careful attention to layout. In any piece of business correspondence, you want clarity, and the impression of clarity is enhanced by an attractive arrangement of the letter or memo on the page. Leave generous margins—at least 1″ on all sides, and place the printed material as near as possible to the vertical centre of the page. Try not to crowd your letter or memo too close to the top of the page; space your letter so that approximately half of the print falls within the lower half of the page.

As the Reference Guide in Figure 3.5 on page 44 indicates, the main difference in letter format is in indentation: in full block style, everything, including paragraphs, begins at the left margin of the page. This makes it easier to type. Paragraph divisions are indicated by skipped lines. In semiblock, the return address, date, complimentary closing, signature, and typed name are indented so that they begin at approximately the centre of the page. Each paragraph is also indented. It has a more balanced appearance, but is also more difficult to type. Modified semiblock uses the same placement of return address, date, and closing as the semiblock, but begins all paragraphs at the left margin instead of indenting. Though the full block style is the most modern, use the style your employer prefers. The memo's heading section is normally arranged at the left margin, usually in the order To, From, Date, and Subject, or Re, though there is some variation to this standard order.

Figures 3.6 through 3.10 on pages 45 to 49 are examples of each of these formats. Note the use of punctuation in these letters: some use open (no) punctuation at line ends; some use closed punctuation, with a colon following the salutation and a comma after the complimentary closing. Either punctuation style is acceptable in any of the formats, but do not mix open and closed styles within a single letter.

MEMORANDUM

DATE:
TO:
FROM:
SUBJECT:

MEMORANDUM

TO: DATE:

FROM: SUBJECT:

MEMORANDUM

TO:
FROM: DATE:

RE:

Dear _____:
Re: _____

Full Block Letter

Dear _____:
Re: _____

Semiblock Letter

Dear _____:
Re: _____

Modified
Semiblock Letter

Figure 3.5 *A handy reference guide for memo and letter formats.*

980 Main Street
Saint John, New Brunswick
E1G 2M3

January 21, 1989

Michael Cea, Manager
Publishing Division
Communications Corporation
555 California Street
Vancouver, British Columbia
X1R 7H9

Dear Mr. Cea

This is an example of the full block style; note how all
the parts begin at the left margin. Paragraphs are not
indented, and lines are skipped between them.

Also, you will notice that this letter is single spaced,
as all business letters should be. Notice, too, the
optional use of open punctuation in this letter—this
means no punctuation at the end of the salutation or the
complimentary closing. Of course, if you wish, you may
retain the colon after the salutation and the comma
following the complimentary closing in this format also.

Sincerely

Abbi Lawson

Abbi Lawson

Figure 3.6 *The basic format of full block style.*

COMMUNICATIONS CORPORATION

555 California Street Vancouver, British Columbia V1R 7H9
(604) 123 4567   Telex 096543782

January 30, 1989

Ms. Abbi Lawson
980 Main Street
Saint John, New Brunswick
E1G 2M3

Dear Ms. Lawson:

    Re: Semiblock Letter Format

    As you will notice, this sample is written in
semiblock style; paragraphs are indented although still
single spaced. Date and closing are also indented,
usually to approximately the center of the page. If this
letter had employed a return address rather than
letterhead, that would also have been indented to the
center of the page.
    The complimentary closing is indented in this
version, and you will also note that I have included an
optional "re" line to specify the subject matter of the
letter.
    As you can see, this version also contains
secretarial notations; these and the "re" line, as well
as the closed punctuation, may be used in any of the
three formats. You may wish to choose any of the three,
but be sure not to mix the styles in a single letter.
Notice that the firm name also appears here, above the
signature.

                  Sincerely,
                  COMMUNICATIONS CORPORATION

                  Michael Cea, Manager
                  Publishing Division
                  Director

MC/jml
encl:2

Figure 3.7 *The basic format of a semiblock letter.*

980 Main Street
Saint John, New Brunswick
E1G 2M3

February 10, 1989

Michael Cea, Manager
Publishing Division
Communications Corporation
555 California Street
Vancouver, British Columbia
V1R 7H9

Dear Mr. Cea:

Re: Modified Semiblock Letter Format

There is one remaining format that we have not yet
discussed. The style of this letter, the modified semiblock
style, shares features of both the block and semiblock
formats.

Note the similarities in layout to the semiblock style,
though here the paragraphs are not indented. This style is
a blend of the other two.

Like both of the others, this one is single spaced and may
use either open or closed punctuation. In this example I
have also used a "re" line to specify my subject matter.
This device may be used in any of the three formats; in the
semiblock format, however, it is indented seven spaces, as
are the paragraphs. Any of the other additions noted above,
such as secretarial notations, file numbers, or corporation
name, may also used in this format.

                              Sincerely,

                              Abbi Lawson

                              Abbi Lawson

Figure 3.8 *The basic format of a modified semiblock letter.*

COMMUNICATIONS CORPORATION

INTERDEPARTMENTAL COMMUNICATION

```
TO:         Michael Cea, Publishing Department

FROM:       Abbi Lawson, Records Department

DATE:       February 14, 1989

RE:         Memorandum Format
```

All memos follow roughly the same format, with the same four components in the heading. Some companies use a ready-made memo form but you can also easily set up your own. Note that the "re" or subject line is very specific. It tells your readers exactly what the memo is about and allows them to deal with it according to their own priorities.

Note that the paragraphs may be laid out in full block style, as these are, or indented in semiblock style, as long as you are consistent within the document. A memo is usually brief; say all you need to say and then stop.

Memos may be signed if you wish; nowadays they frequently are.

Abbi Lawson

```
AL/jml
cc. College English Classes
```

Figure 3.9 *Memo format on a company memo form.*

COMMUNICATIONS CORPORATION

MEMORANDUM

File 0289-MC005

TO: Abbi Lawson   DATE: February 16, 1989
      Records Department

FROM: Michael Cea   SUBJECT: Memorandum Format
      Publishing Department

     As this example illustrates, you may set up your own memo form on a regular piece of typing paper, simply by typing the company name and the word memorandum at the top.

     Note too that the order and arrangement of the heading items may be varied to suit your company's or your department's preference. The paragraphs in this example are laid out in semiblock style, though the body of the memo is single spaced just as in the previous example.

     The coded number at the upper right is a file number, which may be used by large corporations for ease in filing their correspondence.

Michael Cea

MC/jml
cc. College English Classes

Figure 3.10   *Memo created on standard typing paper.*

THINGS TO TRY

SECTION A

The following situations require letters; some of them will carry good news and some bad news. In writing them, observe all of the elements of style and format discussed above. Add any details that might make your letters more convincing.

1. You ordered a black sweater, number JM-2706B, from Contemporary Fashions of Vancouver, B.C. However, the one you were sent is the wrong size; write to the manager, Nancy Schindelhauer, to request an adjustment. Invent any other details she will need to respond to your request. Her address is:

   1729 Trutch Street
   Vancouver, BC
   V6J 7Y8

2. You have read an interesting article on snowshoe making in Canadian Outdoor World magazine; you wish to have more information about the designer, Myrtle Filmore, and about the procedure itself. You are interested in making your own snowshoes, and you wonder whether there are any books or other sources you might consult on the subject. Write to the editor, Ivan Warren, for suggestions. Indicate that you would like to be put in touch with Ms. Filmore. His address is:

   PO Box 103, Station L
   Toronto, Ontario
   M2E 4Z2

3. The mayor and city councillors of your city have finally proposed to build a new parkade downtown. You like to do business in the downtown core, but up to now have generally been discouraged by the lack of parking available. Write to the mayor lending your support to the proposal.

4. You have heard that an old acquaintance of yours has just received the Citizen of the Year award in his or her town; write a letter of congratulations recognizing this achievement.

5. Write to a former instructor or employer, requesting permission to name the person as a reference in a job application.

6. As a summer job, you have decided to offer some form of neighborhood service—painting, cutting grass, house- or pet-sitting, or any other service you can think of. Write an example of the circular you would send to your prospective customers.

7. Ernie Britten worked in your department (Records) at MediaCorp for two years before leaving several months ago. You were one of several supervisors who had the opportunity to oversee his work. He has asked you to provide a reference for his job search, but for your own reasons you do not wish to do so. Write your letter of refusal to Ernie, tactfully telling him that you are unable to write in his behalf. You should not hide behind "company policy," but give your own reasons for refusing his request. Avoid being insensitive or rude, and if possible suggest where else he might seek a reference.

8. You have recently suffered a fire which destroyed a number of the personal effects in your home. Among the items lost are your educational records, particularly your college diploma. You are currently employed at Communications Corporation, but are considering a career move, and you will need the certificate as proof that you graduated from college. Write to the office of the registrar at your college, giving all of the details they will need to locate your file, and inquire whether they will be able to replace your diploma.

9. You work in the Human Resources Department of Communications Corporation, which is accepting applications for a new position; you have been appointed to review the applications and short-list the candidates. One of your tasks is to solicit written references for each of the promising candidates, using the organization's standard reference form. The most promising candidate is Angus MacNeill. Write a letter to his referee, explaining what you need and asking him to return the completed form as soon as possible. His address is:

> Dr. Herbert Hiddle
> Associate Dean of Business
> Hagerstown University
> PO Box 333
> Hagerstown, Indiana
> S7E 6J0

10. You have worked in Communication Corporation's office in Calgary for five years. You enjoy your job, but your spouse has recently been offered a position in Winnipeg. You too have applied and been accepted for a position in that city, and will be moving at the end of June. You have submitted your resignation to the personnel department. You have always been on the best of terms with your supervisor, Phoebe Gerson; she has been supportive to you throughout your employment with the firm and has provided you with promotions and recognition for your special achievements. She has also encouraged you to take additional training and has recognized your potential to move into a management position. You have just recently done so and are sorry to have to leave the company, even though your new position promises to be very rewarding. You wish to communicate your thanks and respect to Phoebe Gerson, and you decide to write her a formal thank you letter. Without becoming too sentimental, but communicating your warmest wishes to her, write the letter you would give to Phoebe Gerson on your departure from Calgary.

11. As personnel manager for Communications Corporation, you have received an unsolicited application for a position in your editorial department from Gordon Gumpley, a former Business Communications Consultant who has also taught writing at the local college. Currently you have no positions available, but you are impressed with the candidate's experience and education. The company has a form letter to answer such enquiries, but you want to give this one the personal touch by sending an original letter to Gordon Gumpley. You want to indicate your interest and your promise to keep his application in the active file. You anticipate a vacancy in your company within approximately six months. Outline the situation and invite him to come in to speak with you if he wishes to do so.

    Gordon Gumpley
    721 Meriel Road
    St. Frances, Ontario
    L6N 4H7

12. You handle adjustments for Contemporary Fashions of Vancouver. Your boss, Nancy Schindelhauer, has forwarded to you a letter from Lucy Peabody (turn to the letter, on page 26 in this book, to review her complaint) requesting an exchange on a sweater she purchased from your Spring/Summer catalogue. She was sent the wrong size in error;

unfortunately, she did not return the sweater within the six week adjustment period your company allows. In fact, she has waited for over three months, and now that particular sweater style is out of stock. Because of this, you are reluctant to replace the sweater, but you wish to preserve customer loyalty (a check of Ms. Peabody's account shows that she is a regular, if eccentric, customer). Recognizing that the original mistake is the fault of your firm, you have two options:

1. You can accept a return of the original sweater, substituting a similar style in the appropriate size, OR
2. You may refuse the return on the grounds that the sweater cannot be resold because the style is no longer carried by your firm, but you may offer Ms. Peabody a voucher good for $10 off her next purchase.

Choose whichever course of action you feel is warranted and write the appropriate letter to Ms. Peabody. Remember that the choice is yours, not hers, to decide.

13. On pages 97–114, you will find a proposal assignment outlining a workshop in Effective Report Writing. You work in Training and Development for Communications Corporation. Your department has just put together the workshop described in this proposal, and you wish to promote it to clients who might be interested in offering it to their staff. One such client, Jacques Angleterre, has used Communications Corporation workshops in his firm before, and you are quite certain he will be interested. Write the promotional letter you might send to Jacques Angleterre to inform him of the new training workshop.

      Jacques Angleterre
      Human Resources Development
      Blackhawk Instrumentation
      1112 Rue Montagne
      Montreal, Quebec
      H2P 8U7

14. The following business letters (Figures 3.11 and 3.12) contain weaknesses. Evaluate them according to the criteria you have learned, and be prepared to rewrite them more effectively if your instructor directs you to do so.

2100 Allendon Crescent
Peachvale, Ontario
L7B 3Z9

July 30, 1989

Ms. Heather Logan
90 Main Street
Oshawa, Ontario
M6K 3D4

My dear Heather

I have just heard the news from Tobias Johnson that your
book <u>Adventures in the Red Deer River Valley</u> has been
accepted by Prentice Hall.

I know just how you feel — I wrote a book myself, you
and I'm sure I'd have publishers just knocking the door
down if I finished it. (They can be so tasteless, can't
they?) But is seems that nearly everyone you talk to is
writing a book these days, it almost makes you think you
should find something original to do!

However, it is an accomplishment, dear — and who knows?
Maybe someday you'll be shaking my hand as a fellow
published author!

Yours very sincerely

Donna Vepier

Donna Vepier

Figure 3.11 *This letter violates the rules for a letter of congratulations. What impression does it make on the reader?*

```
                75 Snayall Drive
                Couchgrass, Manitoba
                R1A 3C6


                October 30, 1989

                Professor L.M. Calvin
                Science Division
                Northwoods College
                Box 456
                Bruce Mines, Ontario
                N0E 040


                Dear Professor Calvin:

                I am writing you this letter to please ask if you would
                kindly act as a reference for me?  I took your class when
                I attended college about 6 years ago.  Now I want to go
                back to school in a similar program at Pineridge College
                here in Couchgrass.  Could you send your letter directly
                to them?  It would be very much appreciated.

                Yours truly,

                M. Jones

                M. Jones
```

Figure 3.12 *How easy will it be for Dr. Calvin to respond to this request? Why?*

SECTION B

Write the following memos, bearing in mind all you have learned about business writing style and format. Add whatever details are required to make your memos convincing.

1. Your class plans an end-of-term party, and you are in charge of its organization. Write a memo to the class outlining the details of the arrangements and contributions, and send a carbon copy to your program chairman.

2. You are Chief of the Records Department of Communications Corporation, and as such are the person who is in charge of keeping data on file. Someone in the Information Management Division (of which Records is a part) has frequently misfiled returned information. The lost data cannot, of course, be easily found. You are not sure who is responsible because so many people use the files, but it could be a superior of yours. You do not wish to discourage people from being helpful, and you certainly don't wish to offend a superior, but you do wish to prevent any further misplacement of documents. Write a memo to all members of the division arranging a solution to the problem. Send a copy to Toby Trapper.

3. Your class is having problems with a particular instructor. You wish to meet with him as a class to discuss the difficulties. On behalf of the class write a memo outlining the specific nature of the problem and requesting a meeting with him to solve it. Watch your tone especially in this one!

4. You are the Parking Supervisor at Waskasoo College. You have received a letter from the transit company in your town complaining of unauthorized parking in the bus zones around the college, which prevents the buses from gaining access to the college stops. This is not the first time such a problem has occurred, and the transit company is threatening to cut off service to the college if it is not corrected. Write a memo to students and staff outlining the problem and requesting their cooperation in correcting it. Direct a copy to Herbert Hoppman, president of the Transit Commission.

5. You are in charge of collecting contributions from your co-workers for the local United Way campaign. Write a memo to all employees encouraging them to contribute enough to meet your goal. Keep in

mind the difficulty of writing this particular persuasive message: people are very reluctant to part with their money!

6. You have worked in the Personnel Department of Communications Corporation for twelve years. You are on reasonably friendly terms with other members of your department, and you are the employee with the most seniority in the firm. One of your co-workers, Ted Dimanche, has been to the hospital for some tests. It has been discovered that he has throat cancer. The people in your department decide to send a gift on behalf of the company, and you have been appointed to solicit contributions from other members of the firm. Write a memo explaining the situation and requesting the donations, outlining exactly how and where they will be collected. Add any appropriate details.

7. After six years as a program designer with Communications Corporation, you have made a number of professional contacts and often hear news from other program designers. A business acquaintance of yours, Ken Franklin, who manages the program designing section of MediaCorp, has passed on to you some information regarding his firm's plans to fully computerize their operation. He has invited Compu-Consulting to give his staff a day-long hands-on training seminar to acquaint them with the proposed equipment. You are aware that the Director of Communications Corporation, Toby Trapper, is considering implementing a similar computerization program, but as far as you know there are no plans for a training seminar. It sounds like a good idea to you, and Ken Franklin is certainly enthusiastic. Write a memo to your boss suggesting that your firm invite Compu-Consulting to provide similar training to you. Explain that the benefits of the training seminar outweigh the costs. Add any necessary details.

8. Your department at Communications Corporation keeps a casual fund for coffee. At present there is a container placed next to the coffee machine into which employees drop twenty-five cents for each cup of coffee they drink. The honor system has worked well in the past; however, recently someone has been stealing money from the container. It is petty theft—usually amounts between ten and twenty dollars—but has begun to cause some friction because coffee is running low and some people have had to contribute more than their share to keep the supply going. It has been suggested at a department meeting that you collect a contribution of ten dollars from each member on the first payday of each month. You can foresee many problems with this proposal

but you have agreed to circulate the information. Write the memo that you send out to all members of the department outlining this proposal and the reasons for it. Keep in mind that despite some suspicions, you have no real evidence as to who the thief is. Though you cannot pinpoint any individual, the practice has to be stopped. Ask for input from all concerned.

9. Your department in Communications Corporation is sponsoring a read-a-thon for charity. Participants will collect pledges from people who agree to donate an amount from twenty-five cents to a dollar for each book read in a six-week period. Participants are required to solicit their own pledges and collect their donations. A list of twelve approved books has been posted in the coffee room. You wish to raise five thousand dollars for the United Way on behalf of the corporation, but you've got to get other employees interested in taking part in the read-a-thon. As an incentive, your department has arranged a prize of a dinner for two at Chez Marietta, the fanciest restaurant in town, with complimentary champagne and theater tickets, along with a limousine ride to the theater. Write a memo that includes all of these details and encourages all employees to take part in this worthwhile project.

10. As Toby Trapper's administrative assistant, you have the responsibility, among other things, for looking after office supplies. You have recently received a box of 1000 memo forms from printing services; the forms have been prepared just as they were designed, except that the word "corporation" has been incorrectly printed as "corporpation." This is not the first such error that you have found in material from that department, and you need the stationery right away. Write a short memo to Enid Spelling in printing services advising her of the mistake and requesting another box of stationery. Direct a copy to Toby Trapper.

11. You are the Chief Executive Officer in Training and Development at Communications Corporation. One of your employees, Carol Mouss, has recently prepared a Training Workshop on Effective Report Writing for Melvyn Tyler of Diehard Industrial Consultants. The Workshop, which is in two three-hour sessions, looks really good and you have agreed that it should be added to the general offerings of the Training and Development department, but you would like to see it expanded to include another three-hour session on Report Presentation (briefings). Write a short memo to Carol Mouss to suggest that she add a section on report presentation to her training workshop. Request that she forward a copy of the expanded course description to you when she has finished it.

12. As a long-standing executive of Communications Corporation, you are a member of the Advisory Committee to the Director, Toby Trapper. Recently, Madeline Spaziani in Public Relations presented your group with a proposal for an in-house magazine which would address some of the more significant problems of information exchange currently facing the Corporation. The group has discussed the proposal fully and is generally in favor of the project, but the major problem is budget. Madeline has asked for approval to hire two employees, at an annual cost to the company of $45,000; unfortunately, budgetary constraints indicate that only one salary can be managed, in the amount of $24,000. As secretary of the Advisory Committee, write a memo to Madeline Spaziani explaining that you would like her to revise her project to meet the limitations of the budget. Suggest that the committee is generally in favor of her proposal, and that it will welcome a chance to discuss a revised version.

13. The following memos (Figures 3.13 and 3.14) are weak for one reason or another. Read them through critically to see what improvements you might be able to suggest. Be prepared to rewrite them more effectively if your instructor requires you to do so.

COMMUNICATIONS CORPORATION

INTERDEPARTMENTAL COMMUNICATION

To: All Employees

From: Margaret Snead, Social Committee Chairperson

Date: July 29, 1988

Re: Arrangements for Annual Company Picnic

This is to inform you that the arrangements for this year's
annual company picnic are final and complete at long last.
After lots of hard work and planning by this committee, it was
decided that it will be on Saturday, August 6.

As you know, we needed to ask for volunteers to lend us various
types of equipment for playing sports and games, and we also
had to arrange for barbecues to be brought to the site.
Luckily we have lots of willing volunteers who can help us out
with these requests and they have agreed to bring their
equipment for us all to use. If you are one of those generous
people who have agreed to volunteer to us any sports or games
supplies or a barbecue or any other kind of item we will be
needing, those who have done so are asked by your dedicated
committee to arrive one half hour early.

The entertainment subcommittee and the food committee,
including myself among many other dedicated individuals will be
on hand by 10 a.m. to get things rolling right along. The
picnic begins properly at 11, though you can plan to arrive
with your family anytime between 10 and 11, unless you are one
of our volunteers mentioned above.

As has been the case with our many previous successful annual
company picnics, this one is to be held as usual at Ellsworth
Conservation Park. If you need directions how to get to the
park, just contact me or anyone else on the social committee.

Plan to bring everyone in your whole family for a super
fun-filled day.

See you all there.

Marge

Figure 3.13 *Convoluted wording makes it difficult to pick out the important information from this memo. How would you improve it?*

COMMUNICATIONS CORPORATION

INTERDEPARTMENTAL COMMUNICATION

```
To:    Members of the Social Committee

From:  Margaret Snead

Date:  July 29, 1988

Re:    MEETING


There will be one more meeting of the social committee
before the big picnic on Saturday to wrap up final
details.

                    Where: Room 2042
                    When:  Thursday, August 4

Please set aside 1/2 hour to attend.

                                    Marg
```

Figure 3.14   *What common error renders this simple message ineffective?*

CHAPTER 4

Informal Reports

As with the other forms of business communication we have studied, reports generally focus on one issue or set of interconnected issues. They can be directed to someone within the organization, like a memo, or to someone outside of it, like a business letter. However, they are generally more formal than a letter or a memo, lengthier and more analytical. They are often commissioned—that is, written at the request of a superior—and are often written in response to a particular problem or situation which has arisen in a company or institution.

Though there are, as you will see, a variety of report formats and styles, all reports share several characteristics with other business writing. Foremost of these, of course, are the Six C's: clarity, conciseness, coherence, correctness, completeness, and courtesy. No business communication can be considered effective without these essentials of style, and in your reports as in all of your writing, you must take care to write and to edit accordingly.

As with other forms of business writing, reports can be either informative or persuasive, and they usually make recommendations for changing or improving a situation or solving a problem. Reports may be either formal or informal, and are used in a variety of business situations. The writer of a report should be sure to use the focusing statement "The main thing I want to tell you is that . . . ," in the first draft. Reports, even more than other business writing forms, usually put the main message first. As well, the report writer must have a clear idea of his or her reader—identified, as you will remember, by needs, expectations, and background knowledge.

The Parts of a Report

Like other business writing, in fact like all other kinds of writing, a report must have a beginning, a middle, and an end—an introduction, a discussion, and a conclusion. But along with these three basic parts, all reports, no matter how simple or complex, no matter how short or long, contain a summary, which precedes the report, and may contain two additional parts: a recommendation or set of recommendations, and appendices. Here are the six standard parts of a report, in order:

Summary   Since reports are longer than most other business communications, and since business people are always busy, the report writer includes a brief statement which gives an overview of the situation or problem dealt with, the general findings, and the specific action recommended. After reading the summary, the reader should know what to expect from the introduction, discussion, conclusion, and recommendations. The substance and the direction of your findings should be clear from the report summary. Further, the language of the summary (along with its introduction, conclusion[s], and recommendation[s]), should be straightforward and clear enough to be understood by the least expert of the intended readers. The length of the summary varies with the length of the report, and though there is no set length, you can think of the summary as being approximately one tenth as long as the report itself. For example, a ten-page report may have a summary of approximately one page, while the summary of a formal report fifty pages long may be five pages. A short informal report using memo or letter format may have a summary consisting of a subject line and a brief initial paragraph.

Introduction   The introduction to a report states as clearly as possible the problem or situation being examined and any necessary background information; it may also set out the writer's approach, assumptions, and the limits of this particular report. In short, it prepares the reader for the discussion of the possible outcomes or solutions offered in the report.

Discussion   The main body, or discussion, of the report sets out the writer's method (including the criteria used to evaluate possible solutions) and the steps that led to the recommendations and conclusions offered in this particular report. It may describe those other possible solutions and show why, according to the writer's criteria, they were judged to be unacceptable. Exactly what you include in this section of the report will depend on what situation you are dealing with. However, if you have detailed technical or specialized data, you would place it here and you may aim your information at the most knowledgeable of your expected readers.

   The discussion is the longest and most detailed part of your report, and may be made up of a number of shorter sections, each with its own heading. The word discussion rarely appears as a heading; instead, it is a broad term that is used to denote everything in the report between the introduction and the conclusion. The headings that are used in the discussion section are specific to the contents of the report. For example, a report that evaluates a training program offered by a local consultant firm might use these section headings:

Program Description
Prerequisites
Advantages of the Program
Costs
Limitations of the Program
Resources

Conclusion or Conclusions   Depending on the situation you are writing about, there may be several possible outcomes or only one. Your conclusions represent the logical results of the investigation or presentation you have dealt with in your discussion. The conclusion lays out any judgments which can be made based on the facts presented in the discussion. There should be no surprises for your reader, who has been led by your discussion to expect this conclusion.

Recommendation(s)   In this section you will recommend what you consider to be, according to your evaluation criteria, appropriate action. You may have one or several recommendations to make. Recommendations normally outline the action that the reader of the report should take and occasionally your recommendation will even list the actions you intend to perform yourself.

Appendices   An appendix is anything that is attached to a report. It is not considered a part of the report itself, but it provides additional support or explanation for points in the discussion. Any relevant supporting information which, for reasons of space or complexity, has not been dealt with in the discussion section of the report may be attached as an appendix. Its purpose is to assist your reader in fully understanding your information. There may be one appendix or several appendices and while not all reports have them, any report may do so. Formal reports are more likely than informal ones to have appendices attached.

Reports, like other business communications, should be carefully planned. Before you begin to write, consult the Report Writing Planner (Figure 4.1). Use it to identify the important elements of your message and the probable needs and expectations of your reader. Jot down the main information to be covered in each part of your report, keeping your reader's needs in mind as you work. Consider carefully the way in which the points in your discussion can be presented, choosing your words with care as you work. Then write your rough draft, beginning with the summary statement. The phrase "The main thing I want to tell you is that . . . " may help you to focus your rough work, but remember to delete it in the final version of your report.

REPORT WRITING PLANNER

Before beginning your report, answer these questions as fully as possible.

1. What is the topic of this report?

2. What is going to be done with this report? Why is it needed? Who asked for it?

3. Who is your reader? What are his or her interests in this subject? What background information is already known to your reader and what will you have to fill in so that your report may be understood and acted on?

4. What is your main message? What will your Summary Statement be?

5. Briefly outline your introduction. Remember to provide the appropriate background information.

6. Outline your discussion; provide any relevant main points and details.

7. Outline your conclusion and recommendation(s).

Figure 4.1 *Use this planner to identify your main message and your readers' needs and expectations.*

Report Situations

Reports can be written in response to a variety of business situations and can serve a variety of purposes. However, most reports fit into one of the following categories.

Investigative/Analytical

The investigative report, which is usually commissioned, examines and/or analyzes a particular problem or question which has been identified by someone in the company. It will probably evaluate causes and effects, and will likely offer solutions to the difficulty. Its conclusions will be based on research, such as results from a controlled scientific experiment, or data collected from a survey or questionnaire.

Evaluation

The evaluation report may be used either on its own to evaluate an existing situation or a proposed action or it may be used as a follow-up report to evaluate recommendations made by another report. Rather than analyzing causes and effects, it usually measures a solution or a situation against a set of criteria in order to determine the suitability or unsuitability of that solution or situation. Its conclusions will be based on a careful comparison between the initial criteria (usually the reader's needs) and the suggested action or solution.

Incident/Occurrence

Written in response to an unexpected (usually problematic) incident, this report is primarily an informative one which outlines details of an unexpected event (an accident, perhaps). It may suggest ways in which the event has influenced work currently in progress and outline the steps which are being taken to correct the setback.

Progress

This kind of report details the progress being made on a long-term project, and may be one of two types. The first, the periodic report, is delivered at regular times intervals—every two weeks, for example, or for very long-term projects, every six months. In a college or school, students receive periodic reports of grades at the completion of each semester. A company's annual report is another example of a periodic progress report. The second type, the occasional progress report, is delivered whenever some significant stage in the project is completed, and the time interval between reports may vary. For instance, if I am working on the construction of a building, I may write reports only when significant stages are completed; since each part of the project takes a different amount of time to complete, my reports will be delivered at irregular time intervals.

Proposals

The proposal is usually initiated by the writer, and is intended to persuade the reader to do what the writer thinks should be done. It might suggest a change that the writer thinks his or her company should adopt (I might write a proposal anytime I wish to create an innovative program in my department) or it might request additional funding for a project that is already in operation. Because a proposal is intended to solicit authorization or funding for the writer's project, it must be sufficiently detailed and convincing to gain the reader's acceptance and approval. A proposal might also be developed in response to a client's request for a service (I might respond to a client's request for a computer training seminar by submitting a proposal for a seminar designed to fit the client's needs).

Any of these situations can call for a report, and the report you write may be either formal or informal in style, depending on the situation, the audience, and the detail of your investigation. Informal and semiformal reports are covered in this chapter, formal reports in the next.

Informal Report Styles

Reports may be presented in any one of several styles. An informal report resembles a memo or business letter that has run to several pages, whereas a formal report may look more like a book manuscript or a formal essay, complete with its own cover and table of contents. Length and layout are the most visible differences between formal and informal reports: the informal report is usually shorter and less detailed than the formal, with an average length of three to five pages; it is usually less detailed, has fewer distinct parts, and a less elaborate layout. An informal report may make use of headings to assist the reader in locating information, but because it is frequently under three pages long, they are not always necessary. In writing your reports, remember that format is meant to serve function.

Choose a format that delivers your message most effectively. Generally, the longer and more complex the report, the more formal it will be, and the more likely it will be to use headings and other organizational devices. The formal report format allows clearer organization of large amounts of material, while short reports may be better presented simply.

As you may already have guessed, reports need not be strictly informal or formal; occasionally you will find that you must write a report that, while important enough to warrant more formal treatment, is not really long enough to require the elaborate formatting of the formal report. Since the organizational structure of the formal report, with its table of contents, special headings, and fancy cover can overwhelm a short report of under ten pages, and a memo or letter format could seem a too casual treatment of your information, you may wish to use a third style of report, the semiformal report, which combines aspects of the informal and the formal report styles. Rather than opening with a memo or letter-like format, it usually has the title, author's name, and date at the top of the first page; it is also more likely than the informal report to use headings to separate report sections. The semiformal report is not really a distinct type, but is a variation of the informal report; it may be used when you wish a more formal appearance for your short reports. In this book we will use the term informal to refer to letter or memo reports, and the word semiformal for short reports that use a more formal style in their opening and on their first page.

Although your employer may sometimes recommend a format for the report you must write, often you must select your own format. How do you know whether to write a formal, an informal, or a semiformal report? Asking yourself the following three questions may help you to decide.

1. What is your purpose? If you are addressing a minor issue, your report will most likely be informal; if the situation is important, your report will be semiformal or even formal.

2. Who is your audience? The more distinguished or the wider your audience, the more formal your presentation should be. A brief document to your immediate supervisor which no one else is likely to read will likely be informal; a detailed proposal being sent to the company president and advisory board, or outside the company, is likely to be formal.

3. How detailed is your analysis? The more complex the problem or issue and the more detailed and thorough your presentation, the more carefully you will have to organize your information, and the more you will require the titles, headings, table of contents, and support materials of the formal report.

In choosing a report format, you should be guided by the complexity of the problem or issue—that is, how much detail and/or research is required—and the intended audience or readers of the report. Most of the reports you will be writing will be informal or semiformal.

Report Forms

In addition to informal and semiformal reports, some jobs require frequent short reports on a regular basis. Such reports may be handwritten on standardized forms provided by your employer or instructor. These forms are used to ensure consistency in cases where large numbers of reports containing similar information must be kept by many people. For example, if you work for an employment agency, you may have to prepare regular client status reports identifying the applicant's background, qualifications, and record of job interviews. Since you would regularly handle several applicants at once and have to keep track of all of them, and since the other placement consultants would be doing the same, your company would probably find it useful to use a special standardized form. Insurance claim forms, student grade reports, and even job application forms are some common examples. Other types which are commonly standardized include occurrence or incident reports, accident or injury reports, and performance reviews.

Nearly any kind of report which is made out on a regular basis could be done on a prepared form. Because the information required is always the same, a form guarantees that each person uses the same format and collects the same details. In this way too, much repetitious work is eliminated. See Figure 4.2 for a sample performance review report.

Informal Reports

The informal report is probably the type of report that you will write most often. Compared to the formal report, it has a more casual format. For instance, it does not have a title page and table of contents. It may be written without enumerated sections, references, or appendices, although any of these could be included if they were needed. Unless your employer provides a standardized form, informal report format is commonly used for

CAREER PROGRESS REPORT

Evaluation for the period _____ to _____

EMPLOYEE'S NAME _____ Department _____

Position Duties: _____

_____

_____

_____

_____

Additional responsibilities since last assessment: _____

_____

_____

_____

_____

Achievements: _____

_____

_____

_____

_____

EVALUATION SUMMARY	Superior	Competent	Developmental
Overall performance	[ ]	[ ]	[ ]
Job related goals	[ ]	[ ]	[ ]
Other goals	[ ]	[ ]	[ ]
Development of other goals	[ ]	[ ]	[ ]
Relationship goals	[ ]	[ ]	[ ]
Potential for advancement	[ ]	[ ]	[ ]
MERIT INCREASE RECOMMENDED		[ ] yes	[ ] no

Figure 4.2 *A useful report form gives clear direction to the writer and ensures a degree of uniformity in subject matter.*

NARRATIVE STATEMENT OF ASSESSMENT: _____

_____

_____

_____

_____

_____

_____

_____

_____

_____

Suggestions for Professional Development: _____

_____

_____

_____

_____

_____

_____

SUPERVISOR: _____ Date _____

Signature: _____

Employee's Comments: _____

_____

_____

_____

_____

I have read this summary and enclosed comments and discussed them with my supervisor.

Employee's signature _____ Date _____

Figure 4.2 *(Continued)*

regular progress reports, incidence reports, evaluative reports, and proposals. If you have been commissioned by your boss to write a short report for his eyes alone, chances are you will be writing an informal report.

Informal reports are typed on one side of the page only, observing margins: 1" at top, right, and bottom, and 1 1/2" at left. The informal report begins as a memo or a business letter. The standard format of the letter (return address or letterhead, date, and inside address) or memo (To, From, Date, Subject) identifies the primary reader, the writer, and date. The subject or re line states the primary recommendation the report makes. If the report is longer than one page, subsequent pages are typed on plain paper. Remember that informal reports, like all other types, may be double or single spaced, depending on the practices of your employer.

An informal report, depending on how long it is, may contain section headings. Each new section begins immediately following the previous one, on the same page. Compare the following list of report parts with the sample informal report which follows.

Contents of the Informal Report

Memo or letter opening

Statement of Recommendation(s) contained in subject or re line

Brief Summary statement

Introduction

Discussion: Background to Issue or Situation

              Outline of Important Facts and Details

              Possible Outcomes, Results, or Solutions

Conclusion

Recommendation(s)

Appendices: (optional)

             Charts

             Supporting Data

             Diagrams

Sample Informal Report

The Situation

Leslie Rousseau is the projects manager of Gwen's Interiors, a decorating firm which has recently been awarded a major contract by Communications

Corporation; the firm is renovating the offices of the director, Toby Trapper, his administrative assistants, and all departmental chairmen. The contract has involved assisting with the selection of new furnishings, choosing new drapes, and installing new carpeting, in addition to wallpapering and painting; it represents several thousand dollars of revenue for the firm. Leslie Rousseau put in a good deal of time with Toby Trapper selecting the specific furnishings and decorating items he wanted. He was particularly specific about the color of his carpeting, and has chosen an unusual shade—Rose Burgundy—which is available only from the Bill Distix Floor Products Company. Leslie has ordered and received the furniture from Gwen's suppliers, and her personnel have been painting, papering, and hanging drapes for two and a half weeks. It is Monday and the deadline for finishing the redecoration is the end of next week. Leslie is well within this deadline, and has just spoken with Toby Trapper on the telephone to assure him that all will be finished in plenty of time. He and his subordinates are naturally anxious to have their offices finished; they are busy and would like to get their workplace back to normal.

All that is left is to install the new carpeting, and Leslie has been assured by the Bill Distix Company that it will be at the Gwen's Interiors plant by the end of this week. On Friday, the carpeting arrives, but instead of Rose Burgundy, Gwen's has been sent Smoky Blue! Leslie telephones the Bill Distix people but they offer little by way of comfort. They tell her that their Rose Burgundy carpeting, currently out of stock, is on back order from California, and they will be unable to fill her order for one thousand square yards for at least another month. Leslie decides to return the carpeting to Bill Distix and approach other firms to see if anyone can fill the order.

Her subordinate, Jerry Purcell, does some checking around, and he is able to secure carpeting of equal quality in a similar shade (Dusky Rose) from Fussbudget Carpet Company; it is five dollars a square metre more expensive than the Distix Carpet, but Leslie will be able to have it by Friday of next week. This means that she will miss the deadline by a few days; Gwen's personnel need three days to lay the carpet, so even if they work over the weekend, the offices will not be completed until Tuesday morning, two working days after the original deadline of Friday.

Leslie's report to Toby Trapper is on pages 76-77 (Figure 4.3). Note how carefully she analyzes the task that faces her: the director is not getting his original choice of carpet, but he will have his offices finished much earlier than would be possible if he waited for Distix. On the other hand, this is an important customer, and he has been very partiuclar about his carpet. Leslie is disappointing him, but she does also have some good news for him. She balances the disappointment with the good news, pointing out that her company is putting his needs first, hence they will absorb the extra cost and work over the weekend to finish by the Tuesday after the deadline. She recommends that he approve the substitution and indicates that she will be cancelling her order with Distix. Note how selective Leslie is about what she includes in her final report. There are many details that she leaves out because her customer does not need to know them. She tells him only what he wants and needs to hear, and puts his interests—and her main message—foremost.

Figure 4.3 is an informal report and because it is going outside the company, Leslie has written it in letter format. If she wished to, Leslie could present this same information in a semiformal report. The impression that she wants to make on Toby Trapper will influence her choice of style.

Semiformal Reports

The semiformal report format may also be used for regular progress reports, incidence reports, evaluative reports, and proposals. Its primary difference from the informal report is the more formal appearance of its first page: instead of using memo or letter format, the semiformal report displays the company name, report title, author's name, and date at the top of the first page, as shown in the sample semiformal report below. It too is typed on one side of the page only, observing the same standard margins as the informal report, and may be double or single spaced, depending on the preference of your employer.

The semiformal report format is used whenever your reports require a more formal appearance than a memo or letter allows. It is also generally a bit longer than the informal report, running usually between five and ten pages, though it can be used for reports up to twenty pages long. Its contents are usually divided into short sections headed with appropriate titles.

Unlike the informal report, where the summary of recommendations is presented in a re or subject line followed by a brief summary statement at the beginning, the semiformal report has a title rather than a subject line, and presents its summary in a short paragraph at the beginning of the report.

Because the semiformal report is a variation of the informal report, the distinctions between them are not entirely clearcut: in some cases the same material can be presented in either format, as in the example below. For a very short report, your choice of format will be influenced primarily by your purpose and your audience's needs. The more important these are, the more likely you will choose a semiformal style over the informal one. If the report is over ten pages long but the issue presented is fairly straightforward and direct, the semiformal format is more appropriate. If your report is likely to be more than ten pages and is divided into many complex sections, you should consider using a formal format.

Contents of the Semiformal Report

Report title, author's name and title, date at top of page one

Summary

Introduction

Discussion: Background to Issue or Situation
                      Outline of Important Facts and Details
                      Possible Outcomes, Results, or Solutions

Conclusion

Recommendation(s)

References/Bibliography (optional)

Appendices: (optional)
                      Charts
                      Supporting Data
                      Diagrams

If Leslie Rousseau wishes, she may make her report to Toby Trapper regarding his office decorations into a semiformal document instead of an informal one (Figure 4.4). Changing the structure this way creates a less casual appearance. Note that the headings Leslie has provided shape the reader's perception of the material she presents. Although the content remains the same, you can see that the change in format creates a very different impression. Compare the appearance of the report on pages 78-79 with her earlier version.

POINTS TO REMEMBER

No matter what kind of report you are writing, you must prepare thoroughly and organize carefully. Remember always to

1. Identify your main message (the main thing I want to tell you . . .)
2. Identify your purpose (to inform or to persuade)
3. Identify your reader (needs, expectations, knowledge)
4. Develop your points fully
5. Observe the 6 C's

GWEN'S INTERIORS

"FOR THE YOU INSIDE"
59 Granville Street, Vancouver V5T 7Y8
(604) 324 5876

April 8, 1990

Toby Trapper, Director
Communications Corporation
555 California Street
Vancouver, British Columbia
X1R 7H9

Dear Mr. Trapper:

Re: Substitution of carpeting for Corporate Office
      Redecoration

Due to an unforeseen setback, I would like to recommend a
substitution in the carpeting for your office
redecoration. The attached carpet sample should assure
you that the shade of this new carpet, Dusky Rose, is
virtually identical to your original choice, Rose
Burgundy, and will match your color scheme
satisfactorily.

When we last spoke about the progress of the project, I
informed you that the decorations would be complete as
planned by Friday, April 15. However, a problem with our
supplier may delay the completion of the project by a few
days.

Bill Distix Floor Products Company has indicated that
Rose Burgundy, available only from them, is currently out
of stock and will be unavailable for at least six weeks.
However, after approaching other firms, we have been able
to secure carpeting of better quality in a similar shade.
We can have this carpeting delivered by April 15, and

.../2

Figure 4.3 *Leslie Rousseau's informal report presented in a business letter format.*

installed in your office by the opening of business on Tuesday, April 19, well before the earliest delivery date we could expect from Distix. The substitution will involve only a few days' delay in completion of the office redecoration.

The new carpet, Dusky Rose, is a better quality carpet costing an additional five dollars per square metre. However, to compensate for the inconvenience to you, Gwen's Interiors will absorb the extra costs. In addition, I am prepared to have my personnel work over the weekend on the installation so that you can be back into your offices by Tuesday, April 19, only two working days later than the original deadline. Given the unavailability of Rose Burgundy, I believe the substitution to be the most satisfactory alternative. If you approve, I will cancel the original order with the Distix company and complete the project with the new carpeting.

Please accept my apologies, on behalf of Gwen's Interiors, for the inconvenience. I will contact you before Friday to finalize the arrangements.

Sincerely,

Leslie Rousseau
Project Manager

Figure 4.3 *(Continued)*

```
                          GWEN'S INTERIORS


              Communication Corporation Office Redecoration

                       Project Status Report

                               by

                  Leslie Rousseau, Project Manager

                         April 8, 1990


     Summary
     Due to an unforeseen setback, I would like to recommend
     substitution in the carpeting for your office redecoration.
     The attached carpet sample should assure you that the shade of
     this new carpet, Dusky Rose, is virtually identical to your
     original choice, Rose Burgundy, and will match your color
     scheme satisfactorily.


     Introduction
     When we last spoke about the progress of the project, I
     informed you that the decoration would be complete as planned
     by Friday, April 15.  However, a problem with our supplier may
     delay the completion of the project by a few days.


     Rose Burgundy is Out of Stock
     Bill Distix Floor Products Company has indicated that Rose
```

Figure 4.4 *Leslie Rousseau's semiformal report. How will her change in format affect the impact on her reader?*

Burgundy, available only from them, is currently out of stock and will be unavailable for at least six weeks. However, after approaching other firms, we have been able to secure carpeting of better quality in a similar shade. We can have this carpeting delivered by April 15, and installed in your office by the opening of business, Tuesday April 19, well before the earliest delivery date we could expect from Distix. The substitution will involve only a few days' delay in completion of the office redecoration.

Substitution of Dusky Rose

The new carpet, Dusky Rose, is a better quality carpet costing an additional five dollars per square metre. However, to compensate for the inconvenience to you, Gwen's Interiors will absorb the extra costs. In addition, I am prepared to have my personnel work over the weekend on the installation so that you can be back into your offices by Tuesday, April 19, only two working days later than the original deadline.

Recommendation

Given the unavailability of Rose Burgundy, I believe the substitution to be the most satisfactory alternative. If you approve, I will cancel the original order with the Distix company and complete the project with the new carpeting.

Please accept my apologies, on behalf of Gwen's Interiors, for the inconvenience. I will contact you before Friday to finalize the arrangements.

Figure 4.4 *(Continued)*

THINGS TO TRY

SECTION A

On the next couple of pages (Figure 4.5) you will find an earlier draft of the report Leslie Rousseau wrote to Toby Trapper to inform him of the problems with his carpet. Compare it with either of the final versions on pages 76 to 79. What changes did Leslie make? Why? Analyze and comment on the revisions, explaining how the final report is an improvement over this draft.

SECTION B

The following report situations vary in complexity and requirements. Whichever report you are writing, observe all of the rules we have discussed, and add any specifications you need to make the report convincing. Before beginning to write, you may wish to use the Report Writing Planner to outline your two principal elements: reader and main message.

1. You work for Communications Corporation. Toby Trapper has assigned you to investigate local charities to which the company might make a corporate donation. The members of the advisory board have agreed to make such a donation, but have been unable to decide which charity would be most suitable. You have been asked to make a recommendation to the advisory group on an appropriate organization, keeping in mind the following information. The company wishes to make a single donation in the amount of ten thousand dollars; it does not wish to make an ongoing commitment to any organization. The organization must be a recognized charity which can issue receipts for tax purposes, and it should not be of a controversial nature which might damage the corporate image. A well-established, respectable charity, one without political connections, would be best. You may consider standard charities such as the United Way, or you may wish to look into making a donation to a local art gallery or educational institution.

2. You work in the public relations department of Communications Corporation. Each year your director, Toby Trapper, arranges an elaborate and carefully-planned company get-together to promote employee involvement and company morale. The evening usually features an informal meeting and an elaborate sit-down dinner, along with an after-dinner presentation which is typically a morale-booster featuring an interesting and inspiring speaker. This year, you were responsible for locating and hiring this speaker and have been able to hire Dr. Dan Ryan, a renowned stress

GWEN'S INTERIORS

"FOR THE YOU INSIDE"
MEMORANDUM

To: Toby Trapper, Director

From: Leslie Rousseau, Projects Manager

Date: April 8, 1990

Re: Need for a delay in office decorations

When we last spoke about the progress of the office
decorations at Communications Corporation, I informed you
that the decorations would be complete by Friday, August
15. Although we have been working well within our
deadline, we recently experienced a minor set-back that
may extend the deadline by a few days.

We have been informed by Bill Distix Floor Products
Company that Rose Burgundy, the carpeting which you
requested, is currently out of stock. However, after
approaching other firms, we have been able to secure

Figure 4.5   *An earlier draft of Leslie Rousseau's report to Toby Trapper. What makes this version inferior to either of the other two?*

carpeting of better quality in a similar shade (Dusky Rose). You will get this carpeting before the earliest delivery date we could expect from Distix. Attached is a swatch of the new carpeting.

The Dusky Rose carpeting is five dollars /m^2 more expensive than the Rose Burgundy. However, Gwen's Interiors is prepared to absorb the extra costs. We will receive the carpeting by next Friday, the day of the original deadline. My personnel will need three days to lay the carpet.

We will work over the weekend, and your offices should be complete by no later than Tuesday, April 19. The order from Distix company will be cancelled. I hope this substitution meets with your approval and regret any inconvenience the delay will cause.

Figure 4.5 *(Continued)*

expert from Vancouver, to speak on the effects of stress in the workplace. From previewing his presentation, you know him to be a dynamic speaker, and everyone, including Toby Trapper, is looking forward to hearing his presentation. You made the arrangements two months ago; the dinner is one week from Friday. Late Thursday evening, just before you leave the office, you receive a long-distance telephone call from Dr. Ryan's agent in Vancouver. Unfortunately, Dr. Ryan has come down with a severe case of strep throat, complicated by laryngitis. He is unable to utter a sound and his doctor has advised him to cancel all of his speaking engagements for at least a week. He will thus be unable to appear at the Communications Corporation dinner.

Despite the lateness of the hour, you immediately contact an acquaintance, David McCarthy, a member of the local library board; you are aware that the board maintains a "Speaker's Bureau" listing of local experts who will speak to community groups for a nominal fee. McCarthy is sure that you will be able to replace Dr. Ryan with another competent speaker, and mentions a speaker who has successfully led seminars for the library board on effective morale-building, another subject of interest to Toby Trapper. McCarthy agrees to contact the new speaker, Dennis Johnson, and to get back to you sometime the next morning with Mr. Johnson's answer; he is reasonably certain that the man will accept. Note that because Mr. Johnson is local, there would be no airfare to pay to bring him to your city to speak. Also, since you have not heard him speak before, you will want to arrange to meet with him to determine the quality of his presentation.

Write the report notifying Toby Trapper of the situation and of your actions. Keep in mind the importance of the evening to the company, and the fact that Toby Trapper has been looking forward to hearing Dr. Ryan speak.

Here is some other information you might need:

TOTAL COST OF PRESENTATIONS

Dr. Ryan:		*Mr. Johnson:*	
Speaker's fee	$1000.00	Speaker's fee	$600.00
Return airfare	799.00	Mileage	30.00
Hotel accommodation (2 nights)	210.00		
Meals & expenses	200.00		
TOTAL	$2209.00		$630.00

3. You are a senior editor in the publishing department of Communications Corporation. Tim Turner, one of the authors for whom you have already

edited a book, has written and submitted his second manuscript, a manual on resume writing. After previewing the manuscript, which he submitted last December, you felt that it was a bit short on examples of effective and ineffective resumes; as well, after consultation with your supervisor, Michael Cea, you suggested that Turner add a section on application forms and expand his consideration of letters of application. Following your suggestions, he submitted a second, expanded manuscript in April. In the meantime, Michael Cea has assigned you three new projects which have taken priority over the resume manuscript, and has given Tim Turner's manuscript to a more junior copy editor, Kathy Hanford. Kathy removed the materials from your office and began work on the project in August.

Recently she approached you with a few questions regarding the work, and you have discovered that the manuscript she has been editing is not the new, expanded version, but the original one which you and your boss felt was not extensive enough. The book is set for release one year from now, and since the whole editorial process (copy editing, choosing typeface, typesetting, dummying, designing a cover, printing, and assembling) takes nearly that long, there is a chance that this misunderstanding may affect the publication deadline. Kathy has edited the first manuscript to fit as it is into your company's standard 7 1/2 x 10", 128-page format. You and Kathy both feel that the new material has to be added, but the book layout must be replanned in order to fit the standard format.

Write the report you send to Michael Cea to explain what has happened, being careful not to lay blame on Kathy for the misunderstanding. Outline what has happened and what needs to be done now, estimating the anticipated delay in publication. Keep in mind that though your primary reader is Michael Cea, the report will most likely also circulate to Toby Trapper, Director of Communications Corporation.

4. When you are working, you will frequently be assigned long-term projects, some of which will require periodic or occasional progress reports. In most instances, you will have to evaluate your achievements and your failures along the way, indicating how you plan to overcome any obstacles you have met with. This semester, you are enrolled in a Business Writing course, and it is now mid-term. Your task for this assignment is to prepare and submit a short (informal) report to your instructor outlining and evaluating your own progress in the course. The report will include such topics as your initial objectives or expectations, your achievements thus far, any failings or obstacles you have encountered and what you have done (or plan to do) to overcome them, the work which has yet to be done, and your expected grade or performance. You will want to supplement your report with evidence such as mid-term or assignment grades, course projects, and topics covered. Keep in mind that you are not evaluating the course *per se*, but your

own commitment to and progress in the course. Essentially what you are preparing is a self-evaluation report such as you might occasionally be expected to prepare for annual performance reviews on the job.

Although the assignment is intended to focus on your Business Writing course, you may wish to use another of your courses instead. If you want to do this, get the approval of your instructor.

CHAPTER 5

Formal Reports and Proposals

Generally the formal report is more complex and detailed than the informal report. It tackles more difficult problems and analyzes them in greater depth, and must present thorough evidence to support its recommendations. It is usually much longer than either of the other report forms, being anywhere from ten to several hundred pages. You would use formal report format if your subject matter was of great significance to your company, if your readership is likely to be large and/or important, or if your findings are extensive. Usually a project resulting in a formal report will involve several or all of the above considerations. For example, a lengthy report from your department to the president of the company which makes important recommendations for major department changes will most likely be formal.

The Parts of a Formal Report

A formal report, especially if it is to be sent outside the company, is meant to maintain the company's professional corporate image. As such, it must be very attractive and professional. It should be error-free and written on one side of the page only, with standard margins of 1" at top, right, and bottom of the page and 1 1/2" at the left side (to allow for binding). It may be single or double-spaced, according to your company's practice. It has a formal cover which bears the company name, report title, author's name, and date. The parts of a formal report are as follows.

The Cover usually encloses a formal report. It can be either a plain purchased one, or a specially-designed one. If you are buying a cover, don't choose one with a gaudy picture or design. A plain colored, good-quality cover is preferable. The cover, like the work inside, should make as professional an impression as possible, and one in grey, black, or white makes a more dignified impression than a wildly coloured one. Avoid cheap, poor-quality report covers. Spending a little more for a good cover will make a better overall impression. If the title of your report appears on the cover, it should be carefully-chosen to reflect the content; it should be informative, but not too long or too brief. A subtitle may help to clarify the material represented within the report.

The Letter of Transfer or Transmittal may be attached to the outside of the report cover, or bound inside the cover just ahead of the title page. The choice is a matter of preference, and in writing your report you should follow the practice of your company. The letter is a formal business letter from the writer (you) to the person or persons to whom the report is addressed. It should briefly outline the reason for the report, and point out some of its important findings or features. Like all business letters, it is single spaced. If your report is to stay inside your company, you may wish to use a memo form for this letter; if it goes to readers outside the firm, write a proper business letter on company letterhead.

The Title Page containing the name of the company or institution, the title and subtitle of the report, the name(s) and title(s) of person(s) who commissioned the report, the name(s) of author(s) and their title(s), and the date comes next. If you are provided with a cover page format by your employer, use that; otherwise use the format of the sample title page shown in this chapter. The formal report should contain a title page whether or not the title appears on the cover.

The Summary of Recommendations usually precedes the Table of Contents; it is a brief overview of all of the important parts of the report and should include condensed versions of the introduction, discussion, conclusion, and recommendation(s). After reading your summary, even your least knowledgeable reader should have an idea of your findings and your approach.

The Table of Contents listing numbered sections and/or pages on which these are to be found comes next; this page is not considered part of the actual body of the report, and so is not numbered as part of the text. Numbering of the pages of the report usually begins at the Introduction.

The Introduction begins the report proper. It not only introduces the subject matter of the report, but it prepares the reader for the report's particular focus and its findings. It also outlines any necessary background information, states the problem or issue, describes the situation, and sets out any limitations that might have been imposed on the investigation or analysis, as well as giving specifics about the direction that the analysis has taken.

The Discussion, or main body, of the report follows. It sets out the writer's method (including the criteria used to evaluate possible results, solutions, or outcomes), and presents a detailed analysis of the problem, issue, or situation that led to the conclusions and recommendations offered in the report. It should outline the important facts of the situation, including relevant history, details, and examples. As well, it should itemize any possible outcomes or courses of action, indicating the one which is being recommended and detailing the reasons for rejecting the others.

The discussion of the formal report, like that of the informal report, is broken into subsections, each with a specific heading reflecting its contents. The contents of these subsections deal with facts specific to the focus of the report. Exactly what topics you include in your discussion will depend on the situation you are dealing with, but detailed technical or specialized data, aimed at the most knowledgeable of your expected readers, should be placed here. All pertinent facts, arranged in a logical order, are presented. Remember that, as in the informal report, the word discussion denotes everything in the report between the introduction and the conclusion, but is rarely used as a heading in the report itself.

The Conclusion outlines any inferences which can logically be drawn from the material presented in the report; it shows the outcome of the analysis. It briefly summarizes the findings of the report, and should be a natural result or extension of the point of view presented in the discussion. It should not contain any unexpected revelations or outcomes, but should satisfy the expectations created by the rest of the report.

The Recommendation (or Recommendations) spells out the action that the report writer expects will be taken on the conclusions presented. If a conclusion says "this is what I think about this situation," the recommendation says "here's what we should do about it." The recommendation may include several steps that the reader is expected to follow; if so, these should be listed and numbered individually so that they are easy to identify and follow.

The Bibliography (a listing of works cited or references) may also be included, since many formal reports involve some sort of research. This list provides the reader with the information needed either to do further reading on the subject of the report, or to check the accuracy of the writer's interpretations.

Appendices are often necessary in a formal report, since the information presented there is sometimes quite complex; as in the informal report, these attachments may include any supporting data which are either too cumbersome or too complicated to be included in the body of the report. Some examples might include charts, supporting data, or diagrams.

The parts of the formal report are usually arranged in the order listed, and each of the parts (Introduction, subsections of the Discussion, Conclusion, and Recommendations) normally begins with its own title on a new page, almost like a chapter of a book. The pages of the report are numbered, starting at the Introduction; depending on your company's policy, these page numbers may appear in the upper right corner, or centred either at top or bottom of each page.

Remember that part of the effectiveness of a formal report, as of any business communication, depends on its visual appeal, so it is important that your report look professional. Although informal reports may sometimes be hand-written, a formal report should really be typed. Follow an accepted format carefully, and take great care that no spelling, grammatical, or typing errors mar the quality of your report. Make corrections in the same type as you used for the rest of the report.

Formal reports also make use of frequent paragraphing and employ headings and subheadings to assist the reader in following the reasoning of the writer. But it isn't simply a neat and professional format that gives a formal report its visual appeal: most formal reports also use visual aids to present their messages clearly.

Using Visuals in a Formal Report

A well-written formal report should contain straightforward, readily understandable explanations, and sometimes visual aids can make your explanations even clearer. Such visual aids include photographs, line drawings, diagrams, graphs, and charts. Depending on their size and immediate relevance to the text (the written material), they may be placed either in an appendix at the end, or within the body of the report. If they are necessary to the reader's immediate understanding and if they are small and simple enough, visual aids should be positioned close to the appropriate paragraph in the report, preferably on the same page. It is best to number them sequentially (Figure 1, Figure 2, and so on) and to identify them by a title and a brief caption. The report text should refer to the visual aid by figure number or title when discussing the material shown in the visual. If the visual is very complex or if it is not necessary to the reader's immediate grasp of the situation, it could be placed in an appendix. If it is very complex but necessary to the reader's understanding, the complex version could be placed in the appendix and a simplified version placed in the body of the report. Below is a brief description of when and how to use each of these visuals. The examples illustrate a house design, the Olshansky model 980, and its sales figures.

Photographs

Whenever you must describe a site, a scene, or a product to give the reader a clear idea of what the item looks like, there is nothing like a good photograph. A photograph may be color or black and white, and may be reproduced as part of the report or inserted after printing.

In choosing your photo, make sure that it is good quality and clear, with no fuzziness or unnecessary clutter in its composition. Whether you choose black and white or color depends on both your purpose and your budget. Color separations for high-quality printing are expensive, and unlikely to be an option for small reports or those which are required in small numbers. If color is not a necessary part of the information you wish your reader to get from the photo or if you have no money for color separations, a black and white photo may suffice. If you are sending the report to a printer, you can include the photo and have it printed with the rest of the report. This approach is recommended if your report is being reproduced in large numbers. If, however, a limited number of copies is required and the report is simply being photocopied in-house, a better way is to have the right number of copies of the photo made and then to paste them into position in the report. You may decide for yourself how many reports you are prepared to assemble by hand like this. An advantage of this hand-assembly is that it may allow you to use color photographs. You may be fortunate enough to work in a firm which has color photocopying facilities: if so, check first to be sure that the quality of the copies is as clear as you need. Plain photocopying is not good enough even for black and white photos.

Line drawings

When the information a reader needs from the visual is likely to be unclear in a photograph, a simple line drawing may be a useful substitute. A line drawing may be used, for example, to show the design of a company logo, or the package design for a product you are about to produce. These drawings are often used in advertising to illustrate products when photographic illustration would be too expensive. You need not be an artist to do a simple line drawing, but your work must be neat and easy to read. It should be drawn with black ink and clearly labelled, and should be as uncluttered as possible. Below are two line drawings of the Olshansky Model 980, one using line shading techniques which will reproduce clearly and one without shading (see Figures 5.1 and 5.2).

Diagrams

Diagrams are useful if your report explains how something works or is assembled. Diagrams may break down a process into steps or may show the parts or proper use of a piece of equipment. A diagram may even show

THE OLSHANSKY
Model 980
Line drawing without shading

Figure 5.1 *A line drawing is useful for illustration when a photograph is unavailable or unsuitable.*

THE OLSHANSKY
Model 980
Line drawing using line shading techniques

Figure 5.2 *Shading can add depth to a line drawing.*

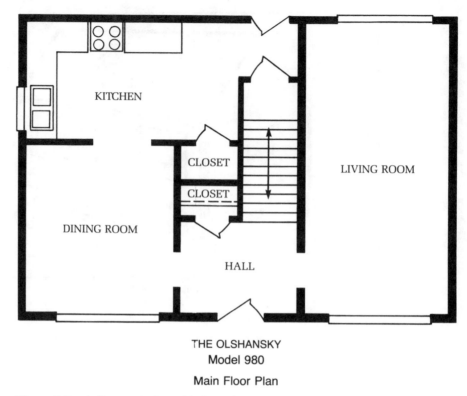

THE OLSHANSKY
Model 980

Main Floor Plan

Figure 5.3   *A diagram such as this floor plan assists your reader in accurately visualizing your meaning and may help prevent misunderstandings.*

the floor plan of the company's proposed new office space. Diagrams, too, should be clearly drawn in plain black ink. Though shading may be used, you should avoid color for both diagrams and line drawings unless your report is being expensively printed. The diagram in Figure 5.3 shows the main floor plan of the Olshansky Model 980.

Graphs

Graphs are used to show the relationship between variables and to display successive changes or growth over time. This growth is shown by a line which slopes either upward (for an increase) or downward (for a decrease) along a scale which is marked out on the vertical and the horizontal axes of the graph. The notches along the horizontal axis (the bottom of the graph) represent time periods (days, weeks, or months), while the notches on the vertical axis (the left side of the graph) show the units which measure the growth (pounds, number of items, or profits). You could, for example, use a graph to track weight gain or loss, showing the time interval along the bottom and the weights along the left side. Graphs may also show a comparison of two or even three growth lines, but any more than three or four leads to confusion. If, when you keep track of your own weight loss or gain, you also record a friend's progress on the same graph, you are using it comparatively. Although colored lines can be used effectively to differentiate tracks on a single comparative graph, you should avoid using color unless you are making only a few copies and can draw all the lines by hand after the report is assembled and copied, or unless your report is being printed in color. Remember that if you try to simply photocopy colors on a standard copier, the colors will all come out black. To compare items in a graph which must be photocopied on a black and white copier, use lines of varying thicknesses or a combination of broken, dotted, and solid lines. The graph below (Figure 5.4) compares the sales of the Olshansky Model 980 with those of two other home models by the same builder.

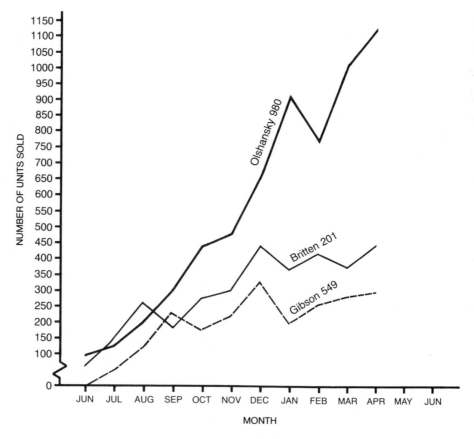

SALES PATTERNS
June 1989 – April 1990

Olshansky 980, Britten 201, and Gibson 549
Models introduced June 1989

Figure 5.4 *A graph enables the reader to easily compare the relative success of the three house models.*

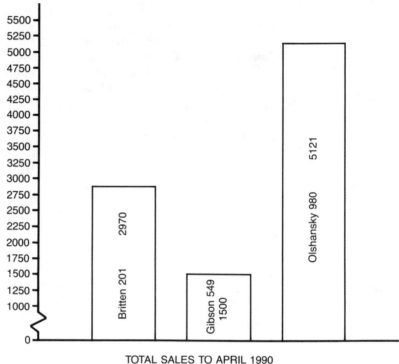

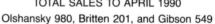

Figure 5.5 *A bar chart can be used to show the sales relationship among the three house models over a particular time period.*

TOTAL SALES TO APRIL 1990
Olshansky 980, Britten 201, and Gibson 549

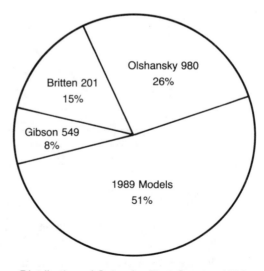

Figure 5.6 *A pie chart shows the relationships of the parts to the whole. The reader can see at a glance what percentage of total sales is represented by each model.*

Distribution of Sales for First Quarter 1990

Charts

These come in many different forms, but the most common are bar charts and pie charts. Bar charts are used to compare a single significant aspect of two or more items; each bar on the chart represents one of the items being compared; the length of the bars may be easily compared and give the reader a quick impression of the difference among items. Bar charts may be drawn vertically or horizontally. The vertical bar chart (Figure 5.5) compares total sales, during the first three months of the year, of the three home models shown in the graph in Figure 5.4.

Pie charts (as in Figure 5.6) are used to show percentages or parts of a whole: how a budget is spent, the percentage of employees who have college diplomas, the breakdown of total business expenditures, or the percentage of total sales made up by sales of one item.

Proposals

In reports, as in all business writing, the writer must develop the skill of identifying the reader's needs, expectations, and interests. As we saw in the section on sales letters, this skill is especially crucial in persuasive writing. A proposal is a report which "sells" an idea, much as a sales letter does. The main parts—summary, introduction, discussion, conclusion, recommendations, and any appendices—are the same as for any other report, and as in other reports, the headings in the discussion section reflect the specific subject matter of the proposal. All reports are challenging to write, but a proposal is more so, because, as the writer, you not only must provide all necessary information, but also influence your reader to accept the project or suggestion you're putting forth. You must focus on the advantages to the reader of the proposal you are offering.

Proposals may be initiated by you, or they may be invited by someone else; your approach will differ slightly depending on which is the case for you. If the idea for the proposal originated with you, you will want to

- Identify your suggestion immediately (remember, "the most important thing I want to tell you is . . .")
- Spell out the advantages of the proposed change. If it will save the reader time, work, or money, or if it will increase sales, efficiency, or profits, show how.
- Make it easy for the reader to implement the proposal. Give all pertinent details of the situation and point out any existing resources that can be put to use. Try to anticipate any questions your reader will have, and answer them in advance.
- Keep an enthusiastic, positive tone, even when outlining disadvantages. Try to express them in positive terms or downplay them. Naturally you

feel that the advantages of your proposal outweigh any disadvantages it may have and your task is to make your reader share this view.

- Indicate as accurately as possible what implementation will cost, but do this after you've presented all the advantages of your proposal. People may be more willing to spend money, time, or effort after they have been convinced of the importance of the project.
- Indicate the steps to be taken to bring about the proposal. Remember that to help your reader accept your project, you must show how the desired end can be achieved.

Above all, with a proposal, you must sound as though you know what you're talking about and have really done your homework. You may know that your proposal is sound, but unless you can convince your reader that you have thought the project through and have anticipated any problems, you will not gain his or her confidence, approval, or money. Don't expect the reader to act on faith if your presentation is incomplete or unclear.

  Occasionally, you will be invited to submit a proposal for implementation of a project that someone else has suggested. As with original proposals, you must still present all the information the reader will need to evaluate your suggestions, but in this case the proposal will differ slightly, since you will be responding to requirements that the reader has outlined for you:

- Since your proposal was requested, you are more likely to have your reader's interest at the outset. However, you will want to emphasize the advantages of your proposal, showing that it is the best means of reaching your reader's desired objectives.
- Because the reader has requested a proposal designed to meet specific needs, you must make sure that the details of your proposal match those requirements.

Remember that a proposal, whether originated by you or written in response to a specific request, must be especially persuasive if you wish to convince your reader to implement the very good idea you are presenting.

Sample Formal Report

Formal Reports may be used for any number of purposes. They may be annual reports, research reports, progress reports, evaluation reports, proposals, or feasibility studies. The sample formal report which follows (Figure 5.7) is a proposal, but the format is similar to that of any other type of formal report.

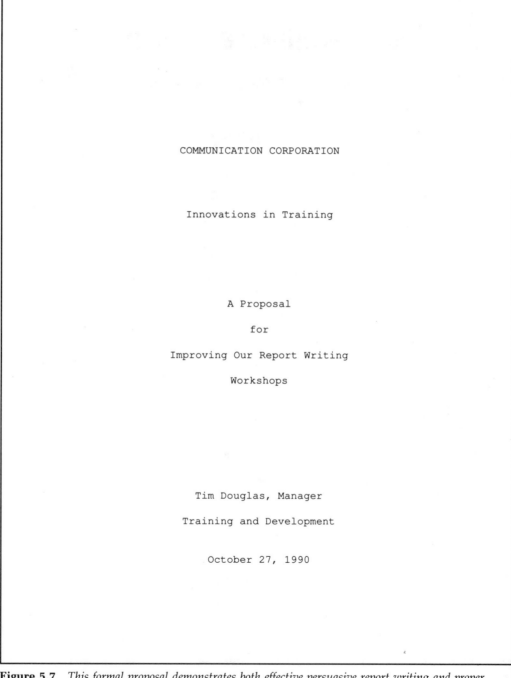

Figure 5.7 *This formal proposal demonstrates both effective persuasive report writing and proper formal report format.*

COMMUNICATIONS CORPORATION

INTERDEPARTMENTAL COMMUNICATION

```
TO:          Toby Trapper, Director

FROM:        Tim Douglas, Manager
             Training and Development

DATE:        October 27, 1990

RE:          Proposed Individualized Training in Report
             Writing
```

I have attached a proposal for the individualized
instruction of Report Writing for new employees, which I
discussed with you in our meeting of October 1. The
proposal outlines the new approach in detail and provides
some samples of the support materials we will need to
implement the project.

My department is prepared, upon receiving your approval,
to go ahead immediately with the design of a manual, and
we expect to be able to begin the new training procedure
as early as March 1991, in time for the spring intake of
new employees.

We would be happy to meet with your advisory group to
discuss this proposal and answer any questions you might
have. We appreciate your interest in our suggestions and
your ongoing support for innovative approaches to
training our employees.

Figure 5.7 *(Continued)*

SUMMARY

A combination of training modules and individual consultations would be a more efficient method of instructing our personnel in report writing than the group workshops we are now using. Since the quality of employee writing is important to us, we want the best training available, and people learn to write best through individual instruction, regular practice, and feedback. Our method would not only provide each trainee with individual attention, but would free the trainer from the repetition of basic material which would be offered in written form.

The proposed new system will consist of a written self-learning package, complete with concrete suggestions for improving writing effectiveness, supplemented with bi-weekly consultations over the initial six-month probationary period. This will replace the two-day seminar which is currently provided. Participants will bring work-in-progress to each meeting with the trainer, who will provide ongoing support and suggestions for improvement. Such a process will obviously require a greater time commitment from both trainer and participants, but should produce more effective and confident writers.

I believe Communications Corporation, as a leader in training and development and a front-runner in the communications field, should implement such a training program in place of the traditional workshop approach currently in use.

Figure 5.7 *(Continued)*

Table of Contents

Introduction 1

Proposal Description 3

Benefits of Individualized Training. 5

Contents of Self-Teaching Manual 7

Preparation and Resources 9

Conclusion 10

Recommendations 11

Appendices

     A. Cost Breakdown for Manuals/Support Materials

     B. Survey Results

Figure 5.7 *(Continued)*

- 1 -

INTRODUCTION

We currently train our personnel in report writing
through a two-day workshop in which one trainer works
with as many as twenty participants. For material which
is primarily content-oriented, this is as effective a
means of training as any, but where mastery of a skill is
required, this is neither the most efficient nor the most
effective means of dealing with staff needs.

Communications Corporation, as a leader in the
communications field, needs employees who are competent,
efficient writers; obviously they must not only
recognize the qualities of good writing, but be able to
produce such writing themselves. Many of the new
employees we hire have strong basic language skills, but
their writing needs polishing. We have long been willing
to provide the support that they need in this area, but
the current system is not meeting all of our needs as
fully as individualized training would.

In present training workshops, for example,
participants discuss writing needs and processes, but
they actually produce only a single short memo report on
a hypothetical situation. There is not room in the

Figure 5.7 *(Continued)*

-2-

workshop for individualized feedback and suggestions, and though participants leave the seminar with basic theory, they are not always able to apply it to their various writing tasks. Many employees feel that though the workshop they attended helped make them aware of some of the weaknesses in their own writing, it did not give them the skills necessary to correct those weaknesses. All agreed that they learned best by doing. Eighty-seven of the one hundred workshop participants we surveyed for this proposal indicated that they would like to have had individual practice and feedback on their writing; only one felt that the present training needed no improvement.

Good writing can be greatly improved by effective editing. To learn how to edit their own writing, our employees need practice and the kind of support that is not available through the present training situation. Though our current method makes employees sensitive to the weaknesses in their writing, it does not offer sufficient help in editing their work to correct these weaknesses. Our proposed training program will offer employees individual editorial appraisal on actual writing projects, and in the process teach them to be better editors of their own work.

Figure 5.7 (*Continued*)

- 3 -

PROPOSAL DESCRIPTION

   Instead of the two-day seminar currently offered to
new employees, the Training and Development Department
would provide each employee with ongoing support for
report writing through two individualized sessions per
month. Each employee would meet with one of the trainers
for approximately one half hour every two weeks over the
first six months of employment. The current workshop
system has two trainers each spending sixteen hours in a
workshop session, with approximately fifteen employees
participating (16 hours x 2 trainers = 32 hours). The
new system would involve a slightly greater time
commitment from our trainers (15 participants x 1/2 hour
x 12 meetings -:- 2 trainers = 45 hours), but less from
each participant (6 hours as compared to 16). Our
proposed training program would take up less of the
employees' time than the current system, but at the same
time would provide them with more effective instruction
in writing.

   Our employees themselves recognize the need for
improved training. Of one hundred employees surveyed,
thirty-six had already attended one repeat workshop
within two years of the first one, and ten others felt

Figure 5.7 *(Continued)*

- 4 -

that they would like to do so. Such repetition is costly to the company in time and money, and doesn't guarantee us the best result. Further, fifty-four percent of our respondents indicated that they spend over half their working time on writing, and most (seventy percent) felt that they relied heavily on others for editorial guidance. An even greater number, (seventy-nine percent) felt that they needed more training and experience in correcting the weaknesses in their own writing.

Clearly, training our employees to be their own effective editors would cut down on the time needed to produce written materials and would improve the quality of work.

Figure 5.7 *(Continued)*

- 5 -

BENEFITS OF INDIVIDUALIZED TRAINING

This system offers distinct advantages over the
current system. The time spent discussing writing theory
would be decreased (we would not, of course, eliminate
the study of theory; that subject would be dealt with in
our self-help manuals) and the time spent assisting
employees in the mastery of writing skills would be
increased. The advantages for participants, training and
development staff, and the company, are as follows:

PARTICIPANTS

1. will receive more practical instruction and more
individualized attention from the trainers

2. will receive immediate and relevant feedback on
actual writing they are doing for the job, and not
on hypothetical examples

3. will receive the hands-on experience necessary
for mastering complicated writing and editing
skills

TRAINERS

1. will be in close contact with participants and
more intimately involved in the training experience

2. will be able to specifically address individual
writing problems which can't be effectively handled
in a workshop

Figure 5.7 *(Continued)*

- 6 -

3. will be able to more effectively track
successful training procedures and techniques
THE COMPANY
1. will gain better trained writers who produce
more efficient writing
2. will experience a reduction in the number of
staff who repeat the report-writing training
3. will benefit from the general morale boost that
is felt across the company as confidence in writing
is increased
4. will benefit from the improved relationships
among staff as they work more closely with the
Training and Development Department

Figure 5.7 *(Continued)*

- 7 -

CONTENTS OF SELF-TEACHING MANUAL

    The bulk of the information needed to produce the training manual has already been prepared by the Training and Development Department; supplementary materials are currently being developed. Below is the projected Table of Contents for the manual.

    Introduction

        The written message

        The basic principles of writing

    Know your reader

        Identify needs

        Identify expectations

        Identify background knowledge

    The "Unnatural" order of Business Writing

        Identify your main message

        The main thing I want to tell you is...

        The business writer's priority list

    Style of Business Writing

        The Six C's

Figure 5.7 *(Continued)*

- 8 -

To Inform or to Persuade:

       Keep it simple

       What's in it for me?

Letters and Memos that Work

       Formats

       Follow your priority list

       Difficult messages

Report Style

       Focus

       Follow your priority list

       Main report parts

Report Formats

       Informal

       Semiformal

       Formal

       Choosing the appropriate report type

Report Situations

       Occurrence/incident

       Evaluation

       Investigation

       Progress

       Proposals

Figure 5.7 *(Continued)*

- 9 -

PREPARATION AND RESOURCES

Present Resources

Oscar Katz, Gwynne Logan, and Heather Scott have already prepared a collection of exercises and tips for use in the Report-Writing Workshop which could, with some minor alterations, be used in an individualized learning program. As well, Gwynne and I have been working on a supplementary manual for participants in the workshops, which should be completed within a month. Some additional materials would have to be developed to round out the package as a self-teaching manual, and these should include a series of guidelines for achieving mastery of specific writing skills.

These learning materials are presently stored on disk and could be set up attractively and printed on the printing department's laser equipment. In-house photocopying and coil binding would enable us to produce economical manuals at under $5.50 each (cost breakdown attached as Appendix A), not much more than the present cost of printing supplementary handouts for the workshops. The manuals could be distributed to new employees on their joining the company, in advance of their first meeting with training personnel.

Implementation Time

Using the existing materials from the Workshop as a starting point, we estimate that the manual and supplementary materials could be prepared within two months, in time to begin the new training procedures for employees hired in the spring.

Figure 5.7 *(Continued)*

- 10 -

CONCLUSION

Though individualized training is not practicable for all of our new-employee programs, we believe it will provide more effective training in professional writing and editing, and ultimately make our employees more efficient and competent writers.

Once the new system is in place for report writing training, we can chart our success by follow-up studies and comparisons with the results of the present method. As well, we might consider making the new manuals and approach available to other companies through our Management Consulting Program. We could of course continue to provide the traditional workshop training to other companies who are interested in it.

Figure 5.7 *(Continued)*

- 11 -

RECOMMENDATIONS

I recommend that the new approach to Report Writing Training be implemented on a pilot basis as of March 1991, for a one-year trial period. At the end of this time Training and Development personnel will conduct a study to determine the success of the project and the feasibility of extending it permanently.

Figure 5.7 *(Continued)*

```
                         APPENDIX A
               Cost Breakdown for Manuals/Support Material
        We recommend having the manuals printed in runs of 50 copies,
   which would help to maintain the cost at under $5.00 apiece;
   manuals will be 48 double-sided pages long.


   First Print Run Cost for 50 Copies
        Laser 'typesetting'  $ .04 per page                 $   3.84*
        Photocopying         $ .035 per two-sided page           84.00
        Binding              $2.50 each                         125.00


   Print Run Total                                          $ 212.84
   Per Copy Total                                           $   4.26


                      Cost of Present Workshop Materials
        Presently there are 50 pages of materials provided to
   participants in the workshop.


   Cost for First Print Run of 50 copies
        Laser 'typesetting'  $ .04 per page                 $   2.00*
        Photocopying         $ .035 per two-sided page           43.75
        Folder               $ .20 each                          10.00


        Print Run Total                                     $  56.75
        Per Copy Total                                      $   1.14


   *One-time only cost; subsequent print runs will come in slightly
   cheaper, since the same typesetter originals can be used again.
```

Figure 5.7 *(Continued)*

APPENDIX B

Survey Results

We used a questionnaire to collect information from 100 employees who have taken the Report Writing Workshop over the last four years. The completed questionnaires are available for viewing in Tim Douglas's office.

1. How much of your working time is spent writing? (Including reports, promotional material, copy, correspondence, or other job-related materials.)

15 respondents spend more than 75 percent of their working time writing; a further 39 spend over half their time on writing activities; 39 said 25-30 percent of their time is spent writing, and 7 indicated under 25 percent.

2. How soon after joining Communications Corporation did you take the Report Writing Training Workshop?

100 percent of respondents had taken the workshop within 4 months of being hired

3. Did the training provide sufficient hands-on experience to improve your writing?

All 100 respondents found the training valuable in making them aware of their writing weaknesses, but 79 felt that it did not give them enough experience in correcting the weaknesses that had been identified.

4. How useful was the hypothetical writing assignment?

96 felt they gained some insight from the assignment, but only 42 felt that there was a direct carry-over to their daily work.

Figure 5.7 *(Continued)*

App. B

5. Would you find it beneficial to do the training a second time? If so, how soon after completing the first workshop?

    46 of the respondents indicated interest in attending the workshop a second time; of those, 36 had already done so within 2 years of the first workshop.

6. Do you presently rely on editorial guidance from others in your department? To what extent would you say this is so?

    70 respondents indicated a heavy reliance—75-100 percent of the time—on guidance from superiors or co-workers; the other 30 indicated a range of reliance from 5-50 percent of the time. Most, however, showed that this dependence decreased as confidence in writing ability increased; usually with more practice the need for consultation diminished.

7. In your view, should the training include more individual consultation?

    All 100 respondents said yes. 80 felt that they would have relied less on peer or superior editorial input if the training had provided more practice with feedback.

8. In what way could we increase the effectiveness of the training?

    7 suggested making repeat workshops mandatory; 5 wanted an additional workshop day; 1 felt the training as it stands cannot be improved; 87 wanted additional individual practice and feedback.

Figure 5.7 *(Continued)*

POINTS TO REMEMBER

Once again, no matter what kind of report you are writing, you must prepare thoroughly and organize carefully. Remember always to

1. Identify your main message (the main thing I want to tell you . . .)
2. Identify your purpose (tell or sell)
3. Identify your reader (needs, expectations, knowledge)
4. Develop your points fully
5. Observe the Six C's

THINGS TO TRY

The following report situations represent some for which you could write a formal report or a proposal. Using the report preparation form in the previous chapter to outline your approach, follow your instructor's directions to write one of these reports.

1. A number of people who are currently employed at Communications Corporation are considering returning to college to enter the program which you are now completing. Toby Trapper has requested a report from you regarding your local colleges' offerings in this area. Investigate the program as offered by three colleges in your area and write up your findings into a formal report addressed to Toby Trapper. You will outline for these prospective students all they will need to know regarding the basics of the program (including admission requirements, duration, courses, any practicum or co-op experience or special courses, advanced standing), as well as the general facilities offered by various institutions (student services, library facilities, recreational facilities, and any special assistance for mature students). You will also want to draw up a study of costs. Evaluate the programs according to their appropriateness for Communications Corporation personnel and recommend the one you feel is most applicable.

2. As Senior Training Officer in the Public Relations Department of Communications Corporation, you have recently been contacted by Toby Trapper, who has received rather disturbing comments regarding the effectiveness of the sales workshops delivered by some of his executive staff. He has had unfavorable feedback from participants in the workshops, and he suspects that many of the executives have had no

training in public speaking. At any rate, their workshop participants have identified flaws in the presentations, such as dull and lifeless delivery, memorized "spiels," and general lack of confidence. Toby Trapper would like you to investigate the situation and offer some suggestions as to how these individuals can improve their report presentations. You have decided to investigate the available resources and have discovered three which seem most appropriate for your people:

1. Dale Carnegie Foundation Training
2. International Communications Training Club (formerly Toastmasters)
3. Public Speaking Course offered by your local college

You will investigate the three options, outlining approximate course content, emphasis, duration of the courses, and cost of each. You have considered preparing an in-house training program as well, and will evaluate the advantages of that program. Toby Trapper has indicated that he wants something done fairly soon and at a modest cost.

3. You work in the Public Relations Department of Communications Corporation's Toronto office. Your company has branch offices all over the country, with major locations in Halifax, Montreal, Winnipeg, Calgary, and Vancouver, and several smaller regional offices in other centres. Toby Trapper, director of the corporation, is committed to team-building and encouraging employee morale.

One frequent complaint you have heard is that there is little continuity of information between branches. As things stand at present, the company has a fairly efficient computer and courier mail system, and information is distributed within departments through numerous memos and other documents. But there is a gulf between branch offices—few of the individuals in the company have any real understanding of what's happening in other branches, and sometimes even in other departments within their own branch.

You are aware that other large corporations publish in-house magazines as a means of drawing everyone in the corporation into the "team". Articles include topics of interest to people all over the corporation, and range from the directly vocational or professional to spotlights on advances in different departments or regions and profiles on individuals within the company.

You believe that such a magazine would go a long way toward improving the morale of Communications Corporation employees, and you feel that the production of such a magazine would be within the scope of your department. You want to produce a glossy, professional publication, on quality paper, and with lots of attractive photos and illustrations. You are aware that Toby Trapper has been looking for some way to recognize the contributions of employees and you think that your magazine could include a feature on these deserving members of the company. Such a periodical would be immensely more attractive and readable than the high number of memos currently distributed and would provide company members with a sense of community.

Since the publishing department has recently acquired a laser printer and equipment for photo reproduction, the magazine could be produced for approximately seventy-five cents per copy, and effectively distributed through the already extensive inter-office mail system. You envision a bi-monthly publication, with a production run of approximately one thousand copies, eight hundred for corporation employees and another two hundred to be used for promotional purposes.

You calculate that producing the magazine would necessitate the hiring of two more staff members to oversee its production, at an approximate cost of forty-five thousand dollars per year to the company, but it would encourage higher morale and ultimately mean greater productivity for the company.

Write the proposal to Toby Trapper encouraging him to authorize you to produce such an in-house magazine.

4. You work in the Training and Development Department of Communications Corporation. Recently Melvin Tyler, a representative of Diehard Industrial Consultants, approached you for advice on training his staff in effective report writing. They prepare much written material, especially reports, but their expertise is not in writing and they need help. He has asked you to prepare a workshop for twenty people which could be delivered in his company by a member of your staff (or even you if you so desire). He has indicated that he wants a workshop of not more than two sessions of no more than four hours' duration each; he can't really afford to have his people spend more than that long away from their regular work.

After clearing the project with Toby Trapper, you set about designing the workshops for Melvin Tyler. You have decided to work in two sessions of three hours each, which could be offered in one day or on two consecutive mornings or afternoons. The topics you have identified for study include

1. Identifying your Main Message
2. Identifying your Reader (Needs, Expectations, Knowledge)
3. Parts of a Report
4. Conciseness and Clarity
5. Informal Report Types and Formats
6. Proposals
7. Formal Report Types and Formats
8. Incorporating Support Data

You have already prepared a booklet at Communications Corporation which would be appropriate for these workshops. It contains materials similar to that in the report chapters of this book, and includes models of effective and ineffective business communication. The sample list of contents given in the training workshop proposal on pages 107–108 provides a helpful model for your workshop contents. It would cost eight dollars per copy. You should outline the methods of presentation you intend to use and in what proportion: you have decided upon a minimum of time spent lecturing and intend to emphasize discussion, small-group work, and individual writing exercises. You have also prepared a videotaped presentation, and you must indicate to Melvin Tyler what equipment the room should have. You will require a room with a blackboard or other form of presentation aid (a flip chart might be acceptable). You will want to indicate also that participants should bring samples of their own writing so that they may receive advice about problems with which they are struggling.

You are planning to provide two seminar leaders so that there will be plenty of opportunity for individual consultation; you have allowed for only twenty participants at a time, and have priced the workshops accordingly. For two of you over six hours, with materials for twenty participants included, you are charging Diehard Industrial Consultants twenty-five hundred dollars.

Write the proposal to Melvin Tyler outlining the details of your workshop.

CHAPTER 6

Oral Reports and Presentations

More and more often, people in business are called upon to present materials orally, whether in workshops, seminars, or staff meetings. Many inexperienced speakers find these public-speaking situations unnerving and try to avoid them whenever possible. However, if you want to advance to a position of authority in your organization, you will sooner or later have to face an audience.

An oral report or briefing, like a written report, should be carefully thought-out, well-organized, and clearly presented. Remember: not only will the actual oral presentations be much improved as you prepare and organize your materials, but your fear will fade as you gain control over your subject matter. Being able to identify the following elements (two of which are important aspects of written communication as well) will help you to control both your preparation and your presentation.

Identify your audience

To whom are you speaking? Are you delivering material to your peers? Your subordinates? A group of visitors? The Board? What is the audience's interest in your project? How much information do they already have? What do they want to know? How much depth do they expect?

Identify your purpose

What are you expected to accomplish in the presentation? Should you give a quick overview of your project? Or should you present an in-depth analysis of your work? Are you expected to outline, support, or justify what you've been doing? Will you be subject to questions from your listeners? What are your own expectations?

Identify the speaking context

How much time are you to be given? If you have prepared a forty-five minute presentation only to find that you have been allotted three minutes, you'll have a difficult time—though not as difficult as if you're in the reverse situation! Make sure you know how much time you're expected to fill. Where are you giving your presentation? How big is the room? What facilities are available? How far will you be from your audience? Will you be using a microphone? Overhead cameras? If you're expected to give a three-minute overview of your project, you may have to do that standing next to your desk as the visitors are paraded through; a forty-five minute comprehensive outline will probably be presented in a meeting room or boardroom.

Types of Oral Presentations

Oral presentations or speeches may be classified into four types:

Impromptu

You are called upon to speak without warning and without any prepared notes. This type of presentation is usually short (under two minutes) and usually on a topic of very general nature.

Manuscript

This presentation is written out and read word for word from the printed document. It is most appropriate in situations where there are legal considerations (a lawyer or politician issuing policy would probably use this form) or where exact wording is important. You may be tempted to use this kind of presentation in other situations, but don't do it. Even if you are very accomplished at reading aloud, you will have trouble keeping your audience's attention during this kind of presentation.

Memorized

A speech can also be prepared in advance and memorized. There is little likelihood that you would be using this approach unless you were acting in a play. The danger inherent in this type of presentation is its tendency, on the lips of any but a highly talented actor, to sound monotonous and flat. Then too, a slip of memory will leave you gasping.

Extemporaneous

This is the most versatile and useful form of oral presentation. The speaker works from an outline written on a card and expands the details from memory. An extemporaneous presentation allows you to respond to the immediate needs of your audience and so establish a bond with them, but also requires detailed planning and organization ahead of time. Of the four types listed here, this is the one that you will find most useful.

Delivery

Organization and preparation are, of course, very important in an oral presentation, but its effect on the audience will also be determined by the quality of your delivery. We all have been bored to near distraction by speakers whose points may have been interesting and even lively, but whose presence was unimpressive or distracting. There are two major aspects of effective speech delivery—sight and sound. The key here is to remember that everything in your speech should enhance and not detract from the overall impact. Often this simply means not calling attention to weak spots, but just as often it means taking special care to create definite strengths in your presentation. Here are some of the factors that can make or break your speech.

Visible Factors: The Sight of Your Presentation

Many people don't realize how powerful a visual impression can be, and in an oral presentation it can be crucial. The speaker may be in front of an audience for anywhere from five minutes to two hours. The attention of audience members is concentrated on the speaker; listeners, without necessarily being completely aware that they are doing so, often take in every idiosyncrasy of the speaker's behavior and every detail of appearance. (To test the accuracy of this point, ask yourself what small peculiarities you have noticed in your instructors—details of behavior, expression, or dress. You'll be surprised how much you have noticed without necessarily being aware of it.) While you can't control everything about your appearance as a speaker, there are some details you can take care of consciously.

1. **Dress for the occasion.**   Wear clothing that is appropriate to the audience and speaking situation. Don't expect to be taken seriously if you show up in a ragged pair of jeans. Even if your presentation is in a class,

dress up a bit. Don't wear clothing you will feel uncomfortable in, and avoid pulling at or adjusting your collar, sleeves, waistband, or any other part of your costume. Remember too, that unless you are speaking about fashion, conservative dress is usually preferable to flamboyant outfits. You want to be memorable for what you say, not for what you wear, and clothing that attracts attention because it is too wild or too sloppy will undercut your purpose.

2. **Stay calm.** Approach the lectern calmly and pause briefly before beginning to speak, so as to give yourself a chance to catch your breath. Don't rush to the podium and immediately begin to speak. Give yourself time to relax and your audience a chance to get used to your presence. Likewise, don't rush away from the lectern just as your last words are leaving your mouth. Give the audience a few seconds to recognize that your speech has ended, and allow for questions if it's appropriate.

3. **Use appropriate movements and gestures to show emphasis.** You should appear calm and self-possessed. Stand straight, but not stiffly, keeping your body weight distributed evenly on both feet, using gestures to emphasize your points. As well, though you will likely feel vulnerable, don't lean on or hide behind the lectern.

   You should not be afraid to move about comfortably in front of your audience, but don't fling your arms about wildly, fidget, or shift uncomfortably from one foot to the other. Such extravagant movements are likely to detract from your presentation (your audience may begin to count your unconscious gestures—Did you notice how many times she pushed her glasses up? Did you see him jiggling the change in his pockets?) If you watch carefully, you will notice that a skilled speaker neither avoids nor overuses gestures or movement. Such a person knows on the one hand how horribly dull it can be to watch someone who does not move at all and on the other hand how distracting unnecessary movements can be.

4. **Maintain eye contact.** The ideal situation is to meet the eyes of every member of the audience at all times—or at least to give this impression! Of course this is an impossible ideal, but if you keep it in mind you will avoid fixing your eyes on a single spot and delivering your presentation to it. Don't, as some speakers do, stare at a point on the back wall (your audience will wonder what you are looking at so intently, and turn to stare too), or look too long at your notes. Eye contact is one of the chief means by which a speaker can create a bond with listeners; it helps to maintain their interest. Don't be afraid to meet your listeners' eyes.

5. **Employ appropriate facial expressions.** People who are nervous sometimes betray their lack of confidence by giggling or grinning inap-

propriately, even when the speech is serious. Try to keep your expression consistent with the material you are delivering. It is perfectly correct to smile when it is appropriate, but you should appear to be in control of your facial expressions.

6. **Use visual aids.** Of course, one of the most important of the visual factors of your presentation is your use of visual aids. When used effectively, these can make your presentation. Remember that they should be simple, readable, and well-timed. More about these below.

Audible Factors: The Sound of Your Presentation

Although in these days of television sound may not be as powerful as appearance, it is still a very significant element in any oral presentation, since your voice is the primary medium through which your information is transmitted. As with visual factors, aural (sound) factors must enhance your presentation and not detract from it. There are some common flaws which first-time speakers are subject to, but with awareness and practice you can eliminate them from your presentation style.

1. **Maintain a reasonable volume.** Most inexperienced speakers speak too softly to be heard. Without yelling, be sure your voice is loud enough to be heard by everyone, especially those in the back row. If you can, practice your speech in the room where it will be delivered, having a friend sit at the very back to determine if you can be heard. If you absolutely cannot project your voice that far, arrange for a microphone to be set up. The members of your audience will not be attentive if they cannot hear you clearly.

2. **Watch your pitch.** A common weakness is for speakers to raise their voices at the end of statements as if they were asking questions. In fact, this voice tic is a form of questioning—a plea for the audience's constant support and reassurance. Avoid sounding uncertain: state your points confidently.

3. **Maintain a pleasant tone.** Voice quality is another factor that can influence a speaker's effectiveness. Try to cultivate a voice that is pleasant to listen to: a voice that is piercing or nasal, for example, may irritate a listener and prevent your message from getting through.

4. **Speak clearly, enunciating your words carefully.** Many speakers swallow the last half of their words, making them hard to listen to or to understand. Check your pronunciation too, particularly of words with

which you are unfamiliar. Mispronunciations of important words will harm your credibility with your audience.

5. **Speak slowly enough.**   Although you don't want to pause for too long between words, far more speakers are inclined to speak too quickly than too slowly. Don't rush through your material. Your audience will appreciate a brief pause here and there to allow them time to grasp your points.

6. **Don't use speech tags.**   Don't say *UM*! (Or *okay, like, you know, really.*) These can be so distracting that an audience may actually begin to count them (Did you know she said "um" thirty-seven times in ten minutes?) and thus lose the thread of your speech. Don't be afraid to simply pause if you need a few seconds to collect your thoughts; you need not make sounds all the time.

7. **Avoid any obvious grammatical errors, any profanity, slang, or inappropriate technical jargon.**   Audiences should be intrigued by your presentation, not put off by it. Slang and profanity are never appropriate, and professional jargon should be avoided unless the audience is made up of people from the same profession. Remember that your most important task is to communicate your ideas to your audience. You cannot do this if your language is inappropriate.

Preparing Your Presentation

Extemporaneous presentations may be most effective in the majority of speaking situations, but like all good reports they require meticulous preparation. You must clearly identify your main message and your audience, but to make the presentation really work well, you must create and maintain an effective relationship with your audience. Your aural and visual delivery will help to ensure that your audience responds to your speech, but your real effectiveness as a speaker will rest on the only written material you will bring with you to the front of the room: your notecard. You should speak from a card rather than a page because, for one thing, its small size forces you to write down only main points, and expand the details from memory as you speak. Unless your speech is very lengthy, (longer than twenty-five minutes) you should try to limit yourself to one card. You may use both sides of the card, but any more will tempt you to write down too much detail. The card is meant to prompt you, and gives you something to rely on should your memory fail you because of nervousness. The use of a card will also force you to extemporize. Preparing your notecard well is one way of ensuring that your presentation will be successful.

You will need to list, in point form, your main ideas. Use words which have enough meaning to you to remind you of what you want to discuss. Then practice your presentation using only the card and your visuals as memory aids. Once you have prepared an outline, go over it again and fine-tune your points so that everything is logical and ordered. Adjust anything that needs to be changed or reorganized. Then make up the final version of your notecard.

Below is a sample outine and note card for a presentation that I gave on the subject of toy design, a hobby of mine and a subject on which I have written and published three books. I initially gave this presentation at the launch of the first book, and have used it since in speaking to other groups on the same topic. Even though I speak in front of classes every day, I was just as nervous in giving this presentation as any speaker is in an unfamiliar situation. Here is how I prepared myself.

Before preparing the outline, I jotted down as many ideas as I could think of that might provide possible approaches to the subject. Here are some of the ideas I came up with.

General Topic   toy design

Possible Subtopics   sources of inspiration for designs
demonstration of a simple technique
steps in the design process
getting designs published
selling your designs
writing a book on design
how I got started designing

Focus

Once I had jotted down several approaches I might take, I thought about the speaking situation. When I first gave the presentation, I was speaking to a variety of prominent people from the college and the community in a large meeting room. The group consisted of about fifty professionals and community members who were not designers themselves, but had come to hear me speak about the book and the design work I was doing. They were interested in learning about the personality behind the work. Their expectations ruled out some of the topics I'd listed; for instance, these people were not interested in getting such a book published themselves. They were not really concerned with learning a technique either, and in any case, the room was too large to allow for such a demonstration, so that was out too. These people were simply interested in learning something about my design work, and my experience had taught me that there are several questions that people often ask about this hobby. For these reasons, I selected three of the above topics: how I started designing; sources of inspiration/ideas; steps in the design process.

I organized my three topics logically, and in my introduction I linked the three by mentioning that these were questions that I was commonly asked about my work in design.

Making the Card

Below (Figure 6.1) is an example of the card I used; note that each of the words is a cryptic signal to me which would trigger my memory of the materials and help me to organize my comments during the presentation.

SAMPLE SPEECH OUTLINE

INTRODUCTION
  Three Questions

I.   How I started designing
      A. Childhood interest
            in toys/crafts
      B. Nephews/Nieces
      C. Altering patterns
            becomes designing

II. Sources of Ideas
      A. Classic Children's stories —
            witches, elves, Santa, gypsies,
            angels
      B. Unusual names —
            Madame Sosostris, Pat Hare
      C. Illustrations — birthday
            cards, coloring/story books

III. Steps in the Design Process
      A. Concept — show birthday card
      B. Sketch — show preliminary sketch
      C. Pattern — show pattern development
      D. Finished toy — show toy

Introduction
  3 Questions
I How I started
      A. Childhood
      B. Nephews/Nieces
      C. Altering + designing
II Ideas
      A. Classic Stories
      B. Unusual names
      C. Illustrations/Cards
III Process
      A. Concept (card)
      B. Sketch
      C. Pattern
      D. Finished toy

Figure 6.1 *The organizational outline for my hobby presentation and the notecard that will serve as a reminder of my main points.*

The words "Three questions" which I used in my introduction reminded me of what I wanted to say to begin my presentation. Because these were questions which were also likely to be in the minds of my listeners, this introduction helped me capture their interest. The points listed under each section developed my presentation fully, and I showed the actual toys as visual aids.

Preparing a Business Brief

On the job you will not be as free to select your presentation topic; instead, you may be required to speak about some aspect of your work. This kind of presentation, often referred to as a briefing, is similar to the kind of presentation outlined above, but may differ in the exact steps you follow to prepare your materials. Let's look at the outline used by Tim Douglas in preparing a briefing for the director's advisory group on the training workshops he outlined in his proposal on pages 97-114 in the previous chapter of this book.

Because Tim's presentation is clearly defined by his work, he already knows the kind of approach he must take, and he does not need to jot down ideas for subjects. However, he does need to clearly define his audience, his purpose, and his speaking context, as suggested at the beginning of this chapter.

Audience

Tim knows that his audience, the director's advisory board, have the power to recommend or veto his proposal. They are an important group in the company, with greater authority than he, as manager of his department, is able to command. They have already received and read his proposal, and have indicated their interest by inviting him to attend their meeting to discuss the proposal and answer their questions.

Purpose

Tim must convince the advisory group that his proposal is worth implementing. He knows that they want to do what is best for the company, so he must show them that this project is to the company's benefit. Because they have already read the proposal, his introductory remarks will be a quick overview of the project, emphasizing the company's need for improved training in this area.

Speaking context

Tim has been allotted a half hour at the beginning of the advisory group's regular weekly meeting. They will be in a small corporate meeting room which holds thirty people. There is no lectern; Tim will be seated at a meeting table with the members of the group around him. It will be a relatively informal setting, and Tim is expected to present a brief introductory presentation followed by questions from the group.

Tim will want to bring support materials with him to the meeting—the survey results, copies of the materials to be used in the training, and an outline of the procedure. He should also prepare a card to help him frame his initial remarks. As a notecard, he can use a shortened version of his proposal, but because his audience has already seen the document, he must not simply read from it or repeat materials they have already read. Given the audience's interests, Tim should emphasize the company's need for report-writing training, the failure of the current system, and the advantages of the new one. Figure 6.2 is the outline Tim developed for his presentation.

BRIEFING OUTLINE

Tim Douglas's Presentation to the Board

INTRODUCTION
   A. The importance of employee writing competence

I. Importance of report writing training
   A. Efficiency
   B. Professional image

II. Problems with current system
   A. Inefficiency   1) Lost time
                     2) Repetition of training
   B. Employee dissastisfaction
                     1) Survey results

III. Advantages of proposed system
   A. Employees
   B. Company
   C. Training staff

CONCLUSION
   A. Implementation plan

Figure 6.2 *Outline for a business briefing. Tim Turner focuses on his audience, his purpose, and his speaking context.*

Visual Aids in Oral Presentations

A good oral presentation is made up of more than a logical, organized outline, however. The impact you make on your audience can be enhanced by the effective use of visual aids. People do learn more easily and remember better when they are shown rather than told something. Visual aids are one of the most effective means of demonstrating a point to your audience. Even a large chart or overhead slide with your main points displayed for the listeners will help to fix your points firmly in their minds. Further, visual aids will not only help make your presentation clearer to the audience, but will serve as an aid to your own memory also. There are several different kinds of visual aids that you can use.

1. If you are discussing an object (such as toys in the example above), bring it with you (if it is large enough to be seen and small enough to be carried around). Having the **actual object** with you will help to attract and hold your audience's attention during your speech.

2. If you can't bring the object itself because of size or unmanageability, you may wish to provide **a scale model**. A small version of the CN Tower or a large-scale model of the DNA molecule will assist your audience in visualizing either, and make your presentation easier to follow.

3. If the object is impossible to bring and no model is available, other visuals such as **pictures, drawings,** or **sketches** may be used effectively.

4. **Charts** or **graphs,** large, simple, and colourful, can also support the speaker.

5. You may even use a **blackboard** or a **flipchart** while you speak.

6. **Films, slides,** and **overhead projections** may also be useful.

7. If your speech discusses how to do something or how something is done, demonstrate the process step by step, using real objects, models, or clear diagrams wherever possible.

Guidelines for the Use of Visual Aids

1. Decide on the type of visual aid (model, demonstration, chart, drawing, photograph, list of main points, etc.) you will employ, and prepare it in advance. If you are using a blackboard, you may wish to write most of your material before beginning your speech.

2. Whatever visual aids you choose, be sure that they are clear and understandable enough to be easily followed by your audience. Complex or

overly detailed visuals will do nothing to clarify the information you are presenting, and may just confuse your audience.

3. Your visuals should be large enough to be seen by your audience. A 3" x 5" photo from your album may be interesting to you, but is unlikely to be of any value to your audience members who cannot see it from their seats. Also it is difficult to keep your audience's attention while you pass around small photos or models. You will want to keep their eyes and attention fixed on you.

4. Show your visual aids while you speak about them (believe it or not, some people forget to show their carefully-prepared charts, drawings, or models at the appropriate moment because of nervousness or poor planning) and be sure to speak about them once you have displayed them. I have seen student speakers display very intriguing-looking visuals and never once refer to them during the presentation. Neither let them take the place of your words nor assume that they speak for themselves.

5. Visual aids should be used sparingly—don't overwhelm your audience with so much visual material that your presentation is lost. Remember that these are aids to your presentation and should not substitute for an effective presentation. The speaker remains the focal point in an oral presentation and all visual aids should enhance that presentation. If you overwhelm your audience with too much visual material it will detract from your presentation. On the other hand, visual aids cannot by themselves serve as a substitute for an effective presentation.

6. While showing your visuals, remember to speak to the audience and not to the picture or chart you are discussing. Avoid turning your back to your audience as you speak so as to maintain your relationship with the audience at all times through your speech. Be especially careful of this point if you are using a blackboard or flow chart as you speak.

7. Practice using the visual aid when you practice delivery of your presentation.

The Importance of Practice

Once you have organized your presentation and selected and prepared your visual aids, the next step is to practice your delivery. If you can, set up conditions as close as possible to those you will be speaking in. Have a friend or someone else you trust listen to your presentation and give you honest feedback. If you have access to a video camera, have your presentation taped and then watch it for ways to improve. You cannot do a really good presentation without practice.

Go over your presentation several times to master your timing, your command of your material, your delivery, and your use of visual aids. Practice until speaking about this topic is as natural to you as breathing. You will have enough to worry about as you step up to speak, without worrying about your command of the material. You will feel much less nervous if you are well prepared, and can concentrate on projecting a positive, confident image. Do not memorize your presentation, however. Your audience will be able to tell, and your presentation will suffer for it.

Practice will tell you whether your presentation fits the time allowance you've been given. Think about how much time you have been allotted: if you have twenty minutes you will need a lot more detail than if you have only five. Practice your delivery, to be sure you have estimated correctly how long your presentation will take. You don't want to be in the uncomfortable situation of having to fill an extra fifteen minutes, or of running overtime.

When you are practicing, do *not* write your presentation out in full. If you do this, you will have a tendency to read it during practice, or to memorize it, either of which will deaden your delivery and almost certainly bore your audience. Practice from the card you intend to use when you finally give the presentation; by the time of the presentation it will be familiar to you and your presentation will be much smoother.

Always practice speaking from the single note card that you intend to use in the final speaking situation.

POINTS TO REMEMBER

In summary, an oral presentation needs as much care and attention in its organization and preparation as a written report. Here, briefly, are the things to remember when getting ready for a presentation:

1. If you can, choose a topic or aspect of a topic that you are interested in and familiar with; in business you will be speaking about some aspect of your work.
2. Focus your topic to suit your audience, according to their needs, their expectations, and their prior knowledge.
3. Tailor your topic and your approach to the purpose and the setting of the presentation.
4. Prepare your topic so you can cover it adequately in the time you have been allotted for speaking.
5. Select and prepare at least one appropriate visual aid.
6. Practice your delivery, practice your use of visuals, practice your timing!
7. Remember that every element in your presentation should support, and not detract from, your presentation. Avoid inappropriate gestures,

mannerisms, or visual items which will distract your audience from the message.

Always remember, whether you are presenting your report orally or in writing, you must prepare thoroughly and organize carefully.

THINGS TO TRY

1. Prepare a briefing on one of the following topics, no more than 10 minutes long and employing at least one visual aid.
   a) Proposal for in-house magazine (see page 116).
   b) Proposal for training workshop in Report Writing (see page 117).
   c) Your research into public speaking training programs (see page 115).
   d) Your research into your program as offered at other institutions (see page 115).
   e) Your research into appropriate charities for a corporate donation (see page 80).

2. Prepare a ten-minute presentation for your classmates, employing at least one visual aid, in which you provide them with tips on one of the following.
   a) Incorporating visual data into a report presentation (briefing or written format).
   b) Applying report-writing organization and how it may be applied to a specific report situation.
   c) Conducting library research for a report on any topic (identify a specific topic, and show samples).
   d) Distinguishing between a proposal and an ordinary business report in purpose and organization.
   e) Writing a self-evaluation report.
   f) Organizing/presenting a briefing.

3. Choose a topic which you are interested in and knowledgeable about, and prepare a ten-minute presentation for your classmates, employing at least one appropriate visual aid and providing some information that your audience is not likely to know already.

CHAPTER 7

The Job Package

Of all of the business writing discussed in this book, the job application package may well be the most important. It is your first venture from school into the business or career world and, because so much depends on the impression your resume makes, it must be as professional—and effective—as possible. Like all other business communication, the job application is prepared with a clear, specific purpose. In it (perhaps more than in any other kind of business writing) you must cater to the needs of the reader. The job application is really a kind of sales document, and the product you are selling is your own suitability for a position in the employer's company. You must focus not simply on what you have done or what you consider most important, but on what your prospective employer wants to hear, and you must tailor your presentation to suit the job you're applying for.

Three parts of the job application will be prepared by you, and there is a fourth part with which you should be familiar. You will be writing a resume, a letter of application, and an application form; as well, you will no doubt have someone write a letter of recommendation on your behalf, so it's important to know what one of these should contain.

The Resume

What is it? A resume is a kind of biographical summary which you prepare for an employer. It outlines the information he or she would likely want or need to know regarding your suitability for a job. You can think of a resume as you on paper—or at least, the professional you—and you want to make the best possible impression. Here more than anywhere else all of the virtues of business writing are important: clarity, correctness, conciseness, completeness, coherence, and courtesy.

Visual impact (layout) makes a big difference as to how you will be perceived. A pleasing balance between white space and print is important; a resume should display its important information without crowding or obscuring any part. Keep in mind that the resume introduces you to the prospective employer, and should make that employer want to speak with you. If it fulfills its purpose effectively, you will be called for an interview. It should make a very good impression.

Types of Resumes

There are three main types of resumes: the functional or skills-oriented, the chronological, and the analytical or crossover. The functional resume is often recommended for people who have little formal education or experience; it emphasizes employable skills instead of positions held or training completed, so it may obscure gaps in an employment or education history. However, there are a couple of problems with this kind of resume. First, its claims are usually unsubstantiated; it contains no dates, names, or locations which can be verified. What is worse is that employers may assume that every functional resume is being used to cover up a sketchy background, because these resumes so frequently are used this way. A sample functional resume is included in this chapter for your consideration, though it may not be the best form to use.

The chronological resume is more widely used and generally accepted than the functional; it presents your training and experience chronologically, always beginning with the most recent and working backwards. The information is divided into categories which are presented under appropriate headings. This organization is usually preferred by employers because it shows the applicant's relevant experience and provides details of dates and names which may be verified.

However, the brief outline provided by the chronological resume alone may not be enough for modern employers. Because the competition for good jobs is always so intense, many employers want more of a "sense" of the applicant before the interview. For this reason, the analytical or crossover resume (which is a blend of the functional and chronological approaches) is often recommended since it combines the strengths of both forms.

Parts of the Resume

What you choose to include in your resume will depend partly on the position you are seeking. Many people assume that a resume should simply list every job-related experience you have ever had no matter what it is. However, since a resume is effective only if it gets you an interview, and it is the reader's needs that will determine who is interviewed, it is very important that the resume be designed and focused to meet those needs.

The following is a broad list of the general categories that may be included on a resume. All resumes should include sections on personal information, education, employment, and skills. The other categories should be selected by their relevance to your experience and the new position.

Personal Information

This should include your name, prominently displayed, your address, and a phone number where you may be reached. You will notice from the recommended examples that this information is displayed in an eye-catching position on the first page. Information such as age, height, and weight, social insurance number, state of health, marital status, and citizenship are no longer considered appropriate for a resume, though in the past they were commonly included. If, despite these guidelines, you wish to include such information, place it near the end of your resume—don't give it a prominent position on the first page. You definitely should not include such sensitive information as religious affiliations, and racial or cultural origin. As a general guideline, leave out any personal information that has no bearing on your ability to perform the job or that may invite prejudice; if a piece of information is not a strength, don't put it into your resume. All you really need here are name, address, and phone number.

Career Objective

This is a phrase or sentence which focuses your career aspirations for prospective employers. The career objective statement is not an essential part of the resume; in fact, a career objective statement that is too vague might even make you appear wishy-washy. On the other hand, a too-firm career objective statement may prevent you from being considered for an alternative position. If your cover (application) letter is well-focused and your experience is very similar to the job you're seeking, you may want to leave out the career objective. Recent graduates of a college program which has trained them especially for a specific type of position may find it unnecessary.

However, a precise, well-worded career objective can focus your background, especially if your experience is diverse. Under these circumstances, such a statement can be useful. There are some instances in which a career objective statement can prove especially useful.

- If you are aiming at a specific position or type of position and are not interested in any other kind of work, you may wish to focus on this aim in your career objective.
- If you have spent some time out of the work force to raise a family, and thus have a gap in your employment history, a career objective can explain this.
- If you are changing careers, this statement can serve as a link between your aspirations and your previous experience.

You will want to be quite clear and specific; avoid such statements as "I am seeking a challenging position which will make use of my skills and offer room for advancement." Can you think of any job to which this would not apply? This kind of vague writing will only put an employer off.

Education

For a student this section usually comes next, because it is your most recent, and likely most relevant, experience. Once you have been working for a year or two, your employment history will be presented first, because by then it will have superseded your education in relevance and importance. Your educational history should include the following information: dates attended, name and location of institution, diploma/certificate/degree obtained, and some detail about your particular program of study. You may wish to mention grades if they are particularly outstanding. List everything back to (and often including) high school, but no further. If you have taken more than one diploma or degree following high school, or if you have been working for a period longer than two years, consider leaving high school out too. Keep in mind that the important thing here is to be selective. The employer needs to know only what is specifically relevant.

Awards

In this section list awards received in school activities in reverse chronological order, giving dates, institutions, and titles of awards. If you have never won any such awards, leave this category out. If your awards are community-related rather than academic, you may want to place them in another category, titled "Special Achievements."

Extracurricular Activities

As with the awards section, use this category to list any significant contributions to school-related activities: membership in academic or athletic clubs or teams, participation in student council, yearbook, or newspaper activities, and so on. If you did not participate significantly in such events, leave this category out. Once you have been working for any length of time, the relevance of this category will fade and you will most likely delete this section too. As a guideline, delete this experience if it is more than three years old, unless your achievements are especially outstanding and have not been superseded by anything else.

Additional Courses/Training

Use this category if you have taken courses which are outside of your actual mainstream education but which have relevance to the job you seek. Perhaps you are formally trained as a mechanic, but have also taken some night school courses in accounting or business management. Perhaps you are a journalist, but have taken some training in computer programming. Perhaps you have taken pilot's training, a CPR course, or training to teach swimming or music. You should not include general interest courses unless they are in some way relevant to your job search. Once again, list in reverse chronological order the dates, institutions, and names of the courses.

Employment History

Beginning with your most recent position, state dates, place of employment, job title, and duties for each position. Provide a quick outline of the job, emphasizing any portable skills you could take to another position. Again, always be forward-looking, keeping in mind the skills needed in the job you want. You may wish to cluster similar or related jobs if you have had a series of them, or to delete some less important or irrelevant jobs. In all cases, emphasize skills which are closest to the job you seek. All jobs have some such skills.

Volunteer Work

If you have held several volunteer positions and feel that they warrant such consideration, you can create a separate category for them; if they are few (and relevant) you might want to include them under your employment history. (However, don't include them twice!) List any positions where you would, under other circumstances, have been paid for your work. Use these only if they contribute meaningfully to your resume.

Community Service

Include membership in service clubs, organization of community events, or civic positions, if they are meaningful. It is usually considered best to leave out organizations of a strictly religious nature. List dates, name, and location of organization, position title, and any relevant duties.

Special Achievements

Include here anything you have achieved which is not covered in any previous section. This section includes awards which are not scholastic in nature (for instance, Citizen of the Year), certification of some form (pilot's licence or swimming instructor's certificate), publication of a book or article, or a special achievement in your work. Once again, in reverse chronological order, include date, name and location of instutition/agency/publisher, and nature of certificate/award/publication.

Areas of Ability/Special Skills

This is is the single most important section of your resume. In this area you have an opportunity to list any useful skills you can provide to an employer, regardless of your past experience. Employers want to know not only that they are hiring someone with the minimum specialized skills provided by training or work experience, but also that this person is the best choice from among applicants who have similar training. It is this part of the resume that may distinguish you from many other applicants of similar background and training. Since it is the best chance you have on a resume to "sell" your unique combination of skills, you should take full advantage of it.

There are many ways in which you can present your skills, but it's a good idea to cluster them under subheadings of some type, as demonstrated in the sample resumes which follow. You will notice a variety in the ways that the skills are clustered and presented in the samples; each person has selected a method which shows his/her skills to best advantage. Choose the format which best displays your skills and experience. Though you may place your skills section at the beginning of your resume, most people prefer to put it at the end where it best supports the information given in the rest of the resume. The prospective employer then comes on it after reading the details of your employment and education history.

Skills are generalized abilities which may be transferred with relative ease from one situation to another, and there are three main areas in which any employer is interested. These classifications will give you an idea where to start from when grouping your own skills.

1. **Specialized** Nearly all jobs require some type of specialized skills which an employer considers necessary to the efficient performance of the job duties. These might be highly technical, such as operation of equipment or machines, knowledge of specific procedures (such as drafting, surveying, or bookkeeping), or simply any ability to do the job. Competence to do the job is obviously desirable. Do you have the skills needed to do the job you are applying for? You should state them clearly on your resume.

2. **Practical** Though these are work-related skills also, they are not so specialized as those in the previous category; instead, they indicate how well you will be able to perform your duties. Many people may be trained, but not all are as competent or reliable as might be wished, and employers want to know that they are getting the most conscientious and reliable people they can find. They want to be assured that you not only can do the tasks set for you, but that you can do them efficiently and well. Some skills that you might include in this category are punctuality, conscientiousness, organizational ability, problem-solving skills, ability to work to deadlines, and efficiency. The emphasis here is on how you handle tasks in the workplace. As you list your skills, be sure you can provide an example of a situation in which you demonstrated this skill. An employer may ask you for such an example in an interview. Claim for yourself only those skills which you can justify.

3. **Interpersonal** The third area of concern for an employer is how well you will get along with your customers, clients, and co-workers. Interpersonal skills include such abilities as tact, diplomacy, leadership, motivational skills, co-operation, and teaching ability. Essentially these skills are concerned with how well you handle your professional relationships with people. Employers do not want sarcastic or complaining people to join their staffs. Again, be cautious about claiming skills you are doubtful about and be sure you can provide examples for any you do identify.

A fourth area which you may wish to consider if it is relevant to your line of work is Artistic Skills; this category might include such areas as drawing, design, painting, and photography.

References

You should prepare a list of the names of people who are willing to provide references for you. Opinion is mixed about whether you should include the names of two or three references in your resume. Some employers I have spoken with are immediately suspicious of an applicant who does not automatically volunteer references, even when he or she promises to supply names "upon request." Others say they are not concerned about receiving the list of references until after the first interview is completed, because they normally do not contact references until that time, and then only if the candidate is to be offered a job. Still others put no stock in solicited references at all.

In light of such divided opinion, what should you do? All of the employers I spoke with agreed that providing references will never hurt your chances, whereas not providing them may do so. It may be safest to provide them if you can.

References are usually former employers or others acquainted with your work, or former teachers. They are not friends, family, or fellow students. Personal references are not very useful to employers, unless a character reference is specifically requested. You will find more information on references in the section on Letters of Recommendation.

Resume Format

The appearance of the resume is also very important. The resume is seen before you are, and you want to make a positive impression on your prospective employer. Few employers will be interested enough to interview an applicant who cannot make an immediate positive impression through the resume; to them a messy resume suggests a lazy or unmotivated individual, which is, of course, not the kind of person they want to hire!

Visual appeal is provided partly by layout. An effective layout creates a pleasing balance between white space and printed elements, with reasonable margins on all sides (1" at top, bottom, and both sides is standard). A consistent format also lends a professional appearance: major headings should begin at a specific margin, lining up neatly beneath one another, and should be presented in the same form (all capitalized, for example, or all underlined). Each subcategory should be indented the same amount, so that they too line up beneath one another against a consistent margin. You should also use consistent spacing between sections: for example, you might skip one line between subsections and two lines between major categories. All this consistency is not only attractive, but, because the layout is also part of your organization, it actually helps the reader to make sense of the information you are presenting.

Use capital letters, underlining, or boldfacing to set apart important details, but use these features consistently and sparingly. A little of each goes a long way and overuse will destroy the effectiveness of these visual devices. For example, if the entire resume is printed in capital letters, it is not only harder to read, but important information no longer stands out. If you have ever tried to read a textbook that someone has attacked overzealously with a highlight pen, you know how quickly the highlighting loses its effect.

It should go without saying that visual appeal also means using a good typewriter or printer, with a sharp, clear, good-quality ribbon. Any photocopies should be perfectly clean.

There are nearly as many varieties of resume layout as there are people to give advice, but these are not all created equal. A good one is easy to scan for important information and should be appealing to look at. Here are some characteristics of an effective resume format. The examples which follow meet these criteria.

1. It maintains consistent margins and uses white space effectively. This means nothing is crowded or cramped, and everything is readable.

2. The main items of information are easily available to the eye, and the reader can skim the resume quickly to get the gist of the applicant's work history without having to read every detail (though necessary details are given too, of course).

3. It is professional in its approach, and flexible in its design, so that it may be arranged to suit an individual applicant.

Never underestimate the importance of an attractive layout; employers can cut down a pile of resumes from two hundred to a short list of twenty by immediately discarding unattractive resumes—without even reading them!

The diagrams below illustrate the use of white space in the resume layout. All of the samples of effective resumes use effective layouts. You can check the effectiveness of a layout by holding the resume away from you. A good layout is appealing to look at even if it is too far away for you to read the print.

Study the diagrams (Figure 7.1) and take a critical look at some of the resume examples to see what makes an effective layout and what looks unattractive.

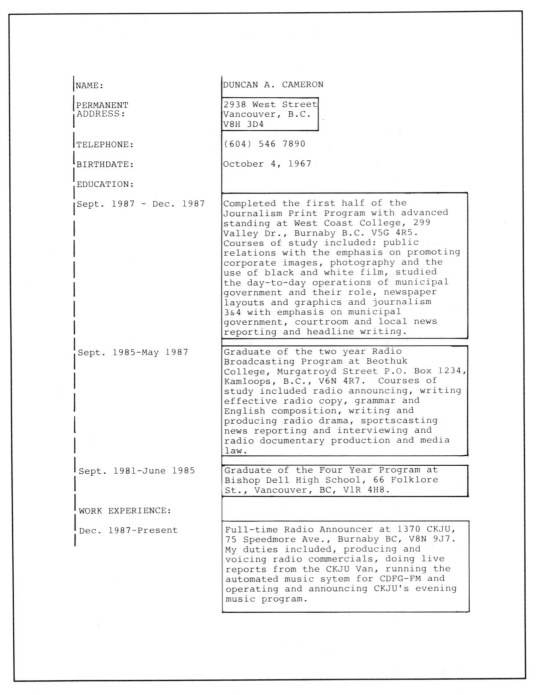

NAME:	DUNCAN A. CAMERON
PERMANENT ADDRESS:	2938 West Street Vancouver, B.C. V8H 3D4
TELEPHONE:	(604) 546 7890
BIRTHDATE:	October 4, 1967
EDUCATION:	
Sept. 1987 - Dec. 1987	Completed the first half of the Journalism Print Program with advanced standing at West Coast College, 299 Valley Dr., Burnaby B.C. V5G 4R5. Courses of study included: public relations with the emphasis on promoting corporate images, photography and the use of black and white film, studied the day-to-day operations of municipal government and their role, newspaper layouts and graphics and journalism 3&4 with emphasis on municipal government, courtroom and local news reporting and headline writing.
Sept. 1985-May 1987	Graduate of the two year Radio Broadcasting Program at Beothuk College, Murgatroyd Street P.O. Box 1234, Kamloops, B.C., V6N 4R7. Courses of study included radio announcing, writing effective radio copy, grammar and English composition, writing and producing radio drama, sportscasting news reporting and interviewing and radio documentary production and media law.
Sept. 1981-June 1985	Graduate of the Four Year Program at Bishop Dell High School, 66 Folklore St., Vancouver, BC, V1R 4H8.
WORK EXPERIENCE:	
Dec. 1987-Present	Full-time Radio Announcer at 1370 CKJU, 75 Speedmore Ave., Burnaby BC, V8N 9J7. My duties included, producing and voicing radio commercials, doing live reports from the CKJU Van, running the automated music sytem for CDFG-FM and operating and announcing CKJU's evening music program.

Figure 7.1 A *A common resume layout with two margins. It is neat but lacks variety. Since the unbroken blocks of print draw the eye downward rather than into the block, important information may be missed.*

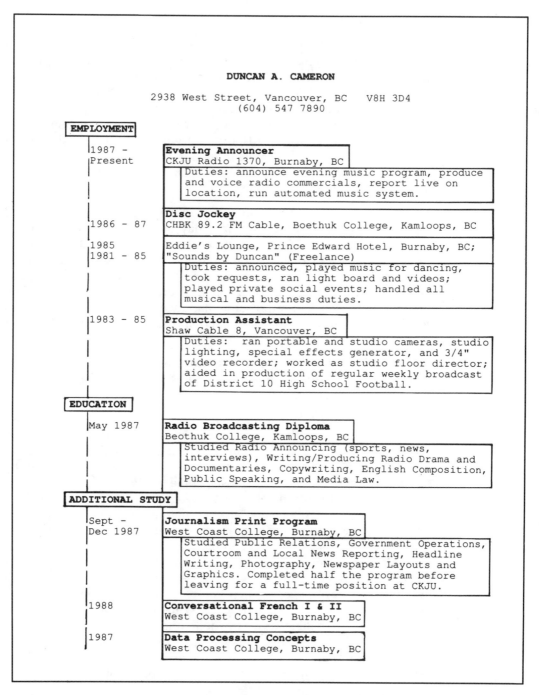

DUNCAN A. CAMERON

2938 West Street, Vancouver, BC   V8H 3D4
(604) 547 7890

EMPLOYMENT

1987 –
Present

Evening Announcer
CKJU Radio 1370, Burnaby, BC

Duties: announce evening music program, produce and voice radio commercials, report live on location, run automated music system.

1986 – 87

Disc Jockey
CHBK 89.2 FM Cable, Boethuk College, Kamloops, BC

1985
1981 – 85

Eddie's Lounge, Prince Edward Hotel, Burnaby, BC;
"Sounds by Duncan" (Freelance)

Duties: announced, played music for dancing, took requests, ran light board and videos; played private social events; handled all musical and business duties.

1983 – 85

Production Assistant
Shaw Cable 8, Vancouver, BC

Duties: ran portable and studio cameras, studio lighting, special effects generator, and 3/4" video recorder; worked as studio floor director; aided in production of regular weekly broadcast of District 10 High School Football.

EDUCATION

May 1987

Radio Broadcasting Diploma
Beothuk College, Kamloops, BC

Studied Radio Announcing (sports, news, interviews), Writing/Producing Radio Drama and Documentaries, Copywriting, English Composition, Public Speaking, and Media Law.

ADDITIONAL STUDY

Sept –
Dec 1987

Journalism Print Program
West Coast College, Burnaby, BC

Studied Public Relations, Government Operations, Courtroom and Local News Reporting, Headline Writing, Photography, Newspaper Layouts and Graphics. Completed half the program before leaving for a full-time position at CKJU.

1988

Conversational French I & II
West Coast College, Burnaby, BC

1987

Data Processing Concepts
West Coast College, Burnaby, BC

Figure 7.1 B *This alternate resume format makes use of more varied margins and smaller print blocks. Important information stands out easily especially if it is boldfaced or underlined.*

POINTS TO REMEMBER

1. Resumes should always be word-processed or typewritten. Even when you are submitting an application in response to an ad requesting a reply in "your own handwriting," you can handwrite the letter—but always type the resume. A typed resume is far more professional-looking and impressive. If you use a word-processor, choose a letter-quality printer or a very good near-letter-quality. Ordinary dot-matrix is not sufficient. Doing your resume on a word-processor will also make revision much easier; you can do your periodic updating painlessly. At the very least, always keep a copy of your previous resume which you can use as a starting place for future resumes.

2. Always use good-quality, white paper. A paper which has a textured surface is especially impressive. You may wish to go with an ivory or grey, and some people use a very pale pastel (though it's not really recommended) but garishly colored papers will detract from rather than enhance your presentation. Most employers are conservative and cautious in their hiring practices, and are more likely to be impressed by a high-quality, well laid-out resume than by a wildly colored one. Make your resume stand out for its quality, and save your flamboyance for after you've got the job.

3. Photocopies must be as close as possible to original quality. If you must send a photocopied resume, make sure it is a clean copy, not smudged or smeared.

4. Don't try to cram too much information onto one page. Length has always been an issue with resumes, and some people sacrifice clarity and visual appeal to fit everything in, producing a crowded, unattractive page that is difficult to read. Though a brief one-page resume may be acceptable for a summer job, most people applying for a permanent position have difficulty displaying their backgrounds attractively on a single page. In a highly competitive job market, you must sell yourself convincingly, and there just isn't room enough on one page to do this.

    One employer, for example, told me that he had recently rejected an applicant for a permanent position because she had not provided enough detail in her resume. He said that if he could offer any advice to her, it would have been, "When you're writing a resume, put some information into it!" A well laid-out, easy-to-skim resume of two pages is, of course, preferable to a crowded, unreadable document of one page. You will want to keep the document from becoming ridiculously long; most professionals can present themselves in no more than three pages. All of the samples that follow are two pages or less.

5. This may seem self-evident, but it bears repeating: a resume should dis-

play your strengths, not call attention to your weaknesses. Use only the categories you require from the above list, retitling them or rearranging them to fit your experience and the job you're applying for.

6. Remember that all dated information in a resume is arranged in reverse chronological order, beginning with the most recent.

Sample Resumes

On the following pages you will find a series of resumes accompanied by brief critiques. The first resume of each pair is weak and in need of improvement and the second is an improved version.

There are several problems with Angela Peterson's first resume (Figure 7.2A). Like most strictly functional resumes, it makes a series of unsubstantiated claims but provides no way for the employer to verify details. No names or locations are given, and the dates are too vague to be helpful. An employer is more likely to be put off than reassured by this sketchy history and will likely wonder what Angie is hiding.

This resume was prepared for Angie by a local agency. In addition to its faults in presentation, it also contains errors in spelling, grammar, and sentence structure. (Angie was educated in Sydney, N.S., not Sidney.) Her unfocused list of skills should be edited toward the job she is applying for, and she would have been better to arrange her lists in parallel grammatic construction (for instance, under "Retail" she could have used verbs throughout, "**sold** clothing, **designed** and **prepared** window...""). Compare this resume to the improved version below.

Angie's new resume (Figure 7.2B) is in analytical format, in the chronological order that employers prefer. The average employer will feel more comfortable about hiring her now; her background can be verified because she's given specific details which provide a basis for her claims. The career objective has been made much more specific and Angie has been selective about the skills she has emphasized, bringing them into line with the job she is seeking. The format is easier to read, with important information prominently displayed. Section headings could be boldfaced or underlined if Angie wished to make them even more prominent. Notice also that Angie's name appears in the centre on the front, but to the right on succeeding pages; this keeps her name in front of the employer reading the document, and also places it in the most dominant position on the page. If she wished, Angie could rearrange this resume to put the "Areas of Skill" first. However, this is not generally considered as valid an approach as the above.

ANGELA PETERSON

1324 Main Street
Red Deer, Alberta
T4N 2D3

Phone 346 1234

CAREER OBJECTIVE

Seeking a position in a people-oriented environment in
which my eagerness to learn and my energetic, responsible
nature will be an asset.

EMPLOYABLE SKILLS

Retail

- sale of clothing
- designed and prepared window and counter displays
- controlled inventory
- priced items
- performed waitress duties

Organizational

- oriented and trained new staff
- organized clothing according to styles/sizes
- filed invoices and receipts

Communication

- adept at verbally communicating with people
- able to be persuasive
- assisted people identify personal choices
- helpful and cooperative fellow worker
- assisted in a promotional advertisement campaign

Figure 7.2 A WEAK RESUME *Based on what you have learned about effective resume content and layout, evaluate this functional resume and point out its weaknesses.*

Angela Peterson

Environmental Activities

- worked on survey crew
- identified tree types and clusters
- determined density and type of trees required for lumber use and environmental beauty
- planted trees

WORK HISTORY

Jean Depot - 1990

Baddeck Lands and Forest - 1989

Ponderosa Steak House - 1988

HOBBIES AND COMMUNITY INVOLVEMENT

Interior design, cooking, sewing, Girl Guide, Air Cadet

EDUCATION

Grade 12 Sidney, Nova Scotia

Computer Programming - 30 hour course

Figure 7.2 A *(Continued)*

RESUME

ANGELA DARLENE PETERSON

1324 Main Street, Red Deer, Alberta T4N 2D3
(403) 346 1234

CAREER OBJECTIVE: A permanent retail career position
requiring excellent sales and organizational
skills and eventually leading to management.

EMPLOYMENT HISTORY:

Aug 1989– Present	Cashier/ Sales Clerk	Consumer Distributing/ Fashions Fabric Ltd. Red Deer, Alberta

Duties include serving customers, handling cash
and credit transactions, keeping track of
inventory, and making bank deposits. I have also
been able to do some window-dressing and
arrangement of creative displays.

Sept 1986– Oct 1989	Childcare Worker (In-Home)	Various Householders Sydney, Nova Scotia

Duties included care of a variety of children,
including some with severe handicaps. I was
responsible for all aspects of the children's
care, including specialized medical treatments,
and did light housekeeping as well.

May 1988– July 1988	Land Survey Crew Member	Lands and Forests Baddeck, Nova Scotia

Under a Canada Works Project, I was one of four
crew members who plotted and surveyed wooded
areas to determine species counts.

Figure 7.2 B IMPROVED VERSION *What makes Angie's improved resume better than the version in Figure 7.2 A?*

Angela Peterson   2

EDUCATION BACKGROUND:

June 1988   High School   Cape Breton AVTC
             Diploma   Sydney, Nova Scotia

             Areas of study included Math, History, English,
             Geography, and Science. Diploma earned.

CERTIFICATES

Feb 1990   Standard   Canadian Red Cross
             First Aid   Red Deer, Alberta

July 1988   Introductory   College of Cape Breton
             Computer Programming Sydney, Nova Scotia
             Certificate

May 1984   Food Handling   Royal Canadian
             Certificate   Air Cadets
                                 Squadron #693

AREAS OF SKILL:

Occupational

             handling cash   processing charge cards
             creating displays   training staff
             soft-selling   knowledge of fashion
              merchandise   trends
             maintaining inventory computer literacy

Personal

             honesty   reliability
             conscientiousness   neatness
             punctuality   willingness to learn

Interpersonal

             salesmanship   tack/diplomacy
             cooperation   sense of humour
             patience   positive attitude

Figure 7.2 B *(Continued)*

Duncan Cameron's first resume (Figure 7.3A) is very disappointing especially since it comes from someone who is actually extremely talented and good at what he does. The format is rather confusing and hard to read, and it contains irrelevant details. Most of Duncan's work history is in some way related to broadcasting, as is his education. He should de-emphasize or delete the irrelevant information to show how he has prepared himself specifically for a career in broadcasting. Notice also that his work experience, which is more recent than his education, should come first.

In the revised resume (Figure 7.3B), Duncan has changed the format and rearranged or deleted some of the unnecessary information to emphasize his training and experience in broadcasting and related fields.

NAME: DUNCAN A. CAMERON

PERMANENT ADDRESS: 2938 West Street
                         Vancouver, B.C.
                         V8H 3D4

TELEPHONE: (604) 546 7890

BIRTHDATE: October 4, 1967

EDUCATION:

Sept. 1987 - Dec. 1987   Completed the first half of the
                         Journalism Print Program with advanced
                         standing at West Coast College, 299
                         Valley, Dr., Burnaby, B.C., V5G 4R5.
                         Courses of study included: public
                         relations with the emphasis on promoting
                         corporate images, photography and the
                         use of black and white film, studied
                         the day-to-day operations of municipal
                         government and their role, newspaper
                         layouts and graphics and journalism
                         3&4 with emphasis on municipal
                         government, courtroom and local news
                         reporting and headline writing.

Sept. 1985-May 1987   Graduate of the two year Radio
                         Broadcasting Program at Beothuk
                         College, Murgatroyd Street P.O.Box 1234,
                         Kamloops, B.C., V6N 4R7. Courses of
                         study included radio announcing, writing
                         effective radio copy, grammar and
                         English composition, writing and
                         producing radio drama, sportscasting
                         news reporting and interviewing and
                         radio documentary production and media
                         law.

Sept. 1981-June 1985   Graduate of the Four Year Program at
                         Bishop Dell High School, 66 Folklore
                         St., Vancouver, BC, V1H 4H8.

WORK EXPERIENCE:

Dec. 1987-Present   Full-time Radio Announcer at 1370 CKJU,
                         75 Speedmore Ave., Burnaby, BC, V8U 9J7.
                         My duties included, producing and
                         voicing radio commercials, doing live
                         reports from the CKJU Van, running the
                         automated music sytem for CDFG-FM and
                         operating and announcing CKJU's evening
                         music program.

Figure 7.3 A WEAK RESUME   What tips could you give Duncan to improve the content and layout of his resume?

Sept. 1983-Present   Part-time service clerk at IGA Markets
                              Ltd. Willow Mall, West Vancouver, BC,
                              V1H 3S8. My duties included, stocking
                              shelves, building displays, assisting
                              customers, bagging groceries and
                              collecting shopping carts.

Sept. 1986-May 1987   Disc jockey, copywriter, and newscaster
                              at CHBK 89.2 FM Cable, Beothuk College,
                              Kamloops BC.

June 1985-Sept. 1985   Disc jockey at Eddie's Lounge at Prince
                              Edward Hotel, 2 Windymere St., Burnaby,
                              BC, V1K 4E3.

June 1984-Sept 1984   Senior Camp Counselor at Camp Marydale
                              day camp, Vancouver CYO, 90 Stiltser St,
                              Vancouver, BC, V8N 1S2. My duties
                              include the supervision and care of 15
                              twelve-year-old boys with one junior
                              counsellor.

Sept. 1981-Aug 1985   Part-time receptionist at St. Joseph's
                              Parish, 409 West 7th Road, Vancouver,
                              BC, V1H 2R4. My duties included, filing,
                              answering the phone photocopying and
                              other odd jobs.

May 1981-Sept. 1985   Freelance Disc-jockey for weddings,
                              birthday parties and other social events
                              at Sounds by Duncan, 2938 West Street,
                              Vancouver, BC, V8H 3D4.

ADDITIONAL EDUCATION:

I have obtained affirmation certificates from West Coast College
for Conversational French Levels I & II and Data Processing
Concepts.

TECHNICAL SKILLS:
From 1983-1985, I was a volunteer production assistant in the
programming dept. at the Burnaby office of Shaw Cable system
Channel 8. During this time, I was trained in the use of portable
and studio television cameras, Sony 3/4" video tape recorders,
television studio lighting, a Sony special effects generator and
as a studio floor director. I also aided in the production of many
shows including the weekly co-producer and as an on-air
commentator.

    Because of my experience from the world of radio

Figure 7.3 A *(Continued)*

broadcasting, I am quite familiar with the setting-up and
operating of various reel-to-reel tape machines, microphones,
cassette machines and public address systems.

HOBBIES AND SPECIAL INTERESTS:

     I enjoy reading science fiction and murder-mystery novels
and listening to music because I have a rather large and
comprehensive record collection. I also play clarinet and bass
guitar.

VOLUNTEER WORK:

     As I've already mentioned, I did two years at Channel 8 and
while I was in high school I got involved with the organization
Youth Across Canada with the Mentally Retarded as well as the St.
Joseph's Children's Youth Organization

REFERENCES:

Adam Marks   Herbert Hiddle
Production Manager   College Instructor
1370 CKJU   West Coast College
75 Speedmore Ave.   299 Valley Dr.
Burnaby BC   Burnaby BC
V8U 9J7   V5G 4R5

(604) 321 5678   (604) 987 5643

Figure 7.3 A *(Continued)*

DUNCAN A. CAMERON

2938 West Street, Vancouver, BC   V8H 3D4
(604) 547 7890

EMPLOYMENT

1987 –   **Evening Announcer**
Present   CKJU Radio 1370, Burnaby, BC
                    Duties: announce evening music program, produce
                    and voice radio commercials, report live on
                    location, run automated music system.

                Disc Jockey
1986 – 87   CHBK 89.2 FM Cable, Boethuk College, Kamloops, BC

1985   Eddie's Lounge, Prince Edward Hotel, Burnaby, BC;
1981 – 85   "Sounds by Duncan" (Freelance)
                    Duties: announced, played music for dancing,
                    took requests, ran light board and videos;
                    played private social events; handled all
                    musical and business duties.

1983 – 85   **Production Assistant**
                Shaw Cable 8, Vancouver, BC
                    Duties: ran portable and studio cameras, studio
                    lighting, special effects generator, and 3/4"
                    video recorder; worked as studio floor director;
                    aided in production of regular weekly broadcast
                    of District 10 High School Football.

EDUCATION

May 1987   **Radio Broadcasting Diploma**
                Beothuk College, Kamloops, BC
                    Studied Radio Announcing (sports, news,
                    interviews), Writing/Producing Radio Drama and
                    Documentaries, Copywriting, English Composition,
                    Public Speaking, and Media Law.

ADDITIONAL STUDY

Sept –   **Journalism Print Program**
Dec 1987   West Coast College, Burnaby, BC
                    Studied Public Relations, Government Operations,
                    Courtroom and Local News Reporting, Headline
                    Writing, Photography, Newspaper Layouts and
                    Graphics. Completed half the program before
                    leaving for a full-time position at CKJU.

1988   **Conversational French I & II**
                West Coast College, Burnaby, BC

1987   **Data Processing Concepts**
                West Coast College, Burnaby, BC

Figure 7.3 B IMPROVED VERSION *Compare this resume with Duncan's earlier one. How is it better?*

Duncan Cameron 2

AREAS OF EXPERTISE

Technical   **Broadcasting Equipment**: can operate all equipment, including splicing/editing and sound effects equipment.

                       Photography: familiar with still and video techniques.

Practical   **Communication**: pleasing professional voice; at ease with public speaking.

                       Organization/Administration: ran my own business; maintain records of all shows produced at CKJU.

                       Reliability/Dependability: displayed as both volunteer and employee.

                       Writing: regularly produce effective copy.

                       Typing: type 40 wpm.

Interpersonal   **Interviewing**: both trained and experienced.

                       Gregariousness: get along well with all types of people.

Artistic/   **General Knowledge**: specialize in musical history, especially twentieth century.

                       Instruments: play clarinet and bass guitar.

                       Acting: have acted in many College productions.

REFERENCES:

Adam Marks   1370 CKJU
Production Mgr.   75 Speedmore Ave
                                       Burnaby, BC
(604) 321 5678   V8U 9J7

Herbert Hiddle   West Coast College
College Instructor   299 Valley Dr.
                                       Burnaby BC
(604) 987 5643   V5G 4R5

Figure 7.3 B (*Continued*)

Although it has a few strengths, Lindsey Goodwin's first resume (Figure 7.4A) isn't very good. Lindsey has a problem background and rather than de-emphasizing the weaknesses (lack of education, series of lay-offs), this resume calls attention to them. As well, negative issues (mentioning any question of a criminal record) and personal issues (his common-law relationship with his girlfriend) should definitely not be mentioned at all. Lindsey says he does not have a record, and counts this as a strength; some employers might wonder why he would even raise the issue! As for his relationship with his girlfriend, it is certainly nobody's business but theirs, and the mention of it might prejudice a conservative employer. The question of marital status should not be raised in any case.

There are other problems here also; since Lindsey has a weak educational background, and especially since it is not his most recent experience, it should not be placed first on the resume. If he mentions education at all, he would be better not to mention what grade he has completed, and just note his attendance at the secondary school. No mention of public school need be made. In any case, his education should certainly follow, not precede, his employment history.

It is also unnecessary (though not wrong) for Lindsey to mention his rates of pay, or his reasons for leaving. He should emphasize his responsibilities more fully and display dates and job titles more clearly too.

Although Lindsey is not a college student, I have included his resume to demonstrate how important it is to tailor your resume to your reader. Lindsey will be seeking a labor job and his resume addresses concerns his prospective employer might have in hiring him. His revised resume (Figure 7.4B) leaves out the irrelevant and damaging material included in the first one, and emphasizes the strengths Lindsey has as a hardworking employee. By deleting the unimportant information, Lindsey is able to fit his resume onto one page, something which is likely to appeal to a busy employer who may not be interested in a lot of paper credentials or minute detail.

RESUME

LINDSEY JOHN GOODWIN
RR # 2 Black Creek, Manitoba

PHONE: 456 7890

PERSONAL:

Date of Birth-December 23rd, 1967   -No physical disabilities
Marital status-Engaged   -No criminal record
Social Insurance No.-765 890 432   -No sick benefit or worker's
Height-5'10"   compensation claim ever made
Weight-175 lbs.

EDUCATION:
Kribsler Public School, 39 Foxx Street, Dundas, Ontario
Graduated from grade eight, 1983
Southfern Secondary School, Southfern Road, Dundas, Ontario
Completed grade nine, June 1984

WORK RECORD:

*Pidgeon Foundry Ltd. 95 Fowler St. Dundas, Ontario
Duties: payloader driving, moulding
Reason for leaving: resigned to move west
Rate of pay: start- $9.51 an hour. finish- $11.84 an hour with
piecework incentive to $17.00 an hour
Dates employed: September 5th, 1988 to January 18th, 1990

* Lunarware, division of Robko Stn. Ltd. 19 Elf Ave. Dundas Ontario
(517) 555 6789
Duties: packing bathtubs and basins, forklift and clamp truck
driving, shipping and receiving. Reason for leaving: shortage of
work (laid off)
Rate of pay: start- $8.95 an hour. finish- $9.61 an hour
Dates employed: February 14th, 1987 to August 17th, 1988

*Pidgeon Foundry Ltd. 95 Fowler St. Dundas, Ontario
Duties: filling ladle, pouring iron, forklift driving
Reason for leaving; shortage of work (laid off)
Rate of pay: $8.91 an hour
Dates employed: August 3rd, 1985 to May 28th, 1986

*Wattles Metal and Covering, Robko Business Park, Black Creek,
Manitoba
Duties: making up work orders for heating duct and custom sheet
metal work. Reason for leaving: company went bankrupt (laid off)
Rate of pay: $6.00 an hour
Dates employed: October, 1984 to January, 1985

Figure 7.4 A WEAK RESUME *What information has Lindsey included that might better be left out?*

ABILITIES:

    -working quickly as well as accurately; have experience on
piecework
-operating lift trucks; have lift truck license
-have St. John's First Aid Certificate

HOBBIES:

    -camping, fishing, gardening, horse back riding
-playing guitar, reading novels
-weightlifting

COMMENTS:

    I was living in Ontario with my fiance. She was offered an
exceptional educational opportunity here in Manitoba which
initiated our move west. I am hard-working, energetic, and
dedicated to my work. I get along well with my fellow workers and
supervisors, although I also excel under unsupervised conditions.

Figure 7.4 A *(Continued)*

RESUME

LINDSEY JOHN GOODWIN
RR # 2 Black Creek, Manitoba

456 7890

WORK RECORD:

1988-90   Driver/Laborer   Pidgeon Foundry Ltd.
1985-86   Dundas, Ontario

           Duties: Driving payloader; casting and moulding metalwork.

1987-88   Laborer   Lunarware Ltd
                                   Dundas, Ontario

           Duties: Forklift and clamp truck driving, shipping and
           receiving.

1984-85   Order Desk Clerk   Wattles Metal and Covering
                                   Black Creek, Manitoba

           Duties: Making up work orders for heating duct and custom
           sheet metal work.

SKILLS:

Work-   - Licensed lift truck operator
Related   - Experienced on piecework
           - Have St. John Ambulance First Aid Certificate

Personal   - Hardworking, energetic, and dedicated to my work
           - Get along with fellow workers and supervisors
           - Able to work without supervision

EDUCATION:

1984   High School   Southfern Secondary School
                                   Dundas, Ontario

AVAILABILITY:

Immediate.

Figure 7.4 B IMPROVED VERSION   *In Lindsey's case, shorter is better. What changes has he made to improve his chances of getting the job he wants?*

Lisa Gimlich's first resume (Figure 7.5A) is a terrible effort for a brand-new college graduate. First of all, she hasn't even provided the reader with a name. Since resumes and letters of application often get separated, your name must be on the document. Also, look closely at the layout. The poor use of white space (everything crowded toward the left, with little distinction between main points and subpoints) and the lack of highlighting of position/program titles make this resume very difficult to read. The applicant has provided no detail about any of the programs taken, and such a lengthy listing of programs started and abandoned gives the impression of indecision; an employer might feel that this person is a quitter.

Note the use of the capital I in place of the numeral 1 (if your typewriter doesn't have this numeral, you should know it's customary to use a lower case L—l—in its place). Also, there are numerous misspellings throughout this resume, and under "Other", our candiate doesn't even tell us what Board of Directors is referred to.

Employers like to see a listing of skills which show a genuine knowledge of the field, something which is lacking here. Originally, this resume was typed on a portable typewriter with uneven lettering, using a faded ribbon. Needless to say, faced with resumes from highly qualified candidates who had put some real thought and effort into their applications, no employer would bother to puzzle through this messy and ill-conceived resume. It's headed straight for the trash.

Lisa's second resume (Figure 7.5B) is much better. She has given herself a better chance to be considered by her prospective employers, not only because she has corrected her errors and improved the organization of her resume, but because she has incorporated some of the language of her profession into her presentation. This is something you should try to do whenever you can; employers of new graduates like to see the applicants correctly using the terms associated with the profession because such usage suggests both knowledge and confidence. Note that Lisa's listing of duties and activities has also been improved, and that she has deleted the long list of programs that made her sound like a quitter.

RESUME

Personal

123 Braemar Way
Forestville, Ontario

555-9876

Education

September 1988
to May 1990

Waskasoo College
Social Service Program
Cedar Falls Campus

September 1982
to January 1983

Waskasoo College
Mini Child Care Course

September 1979
to May 1981

Waskasoo College
Correctional Worker Program
Cedar Falls Campus

September 1980
to May 1981

Waskasoo College
Upgrading Course
Allendon Campus

Field Placement

September 1989
to May 1990
Duties:

Jersey Youth Services
Inner City Youth Program
Referrals, I.D. Verification,
Intakes, Councelling, Groups,
Reception.

January 1989
to May 1989
Duties:

Forestville Volunteer Centre

Community Relations, Recognition
Projects, Interviewing, Church Out-
Reach Projects, Recruitment Projects,
Office Duties.

Work Experience

May 1989 to
present
Duties:

Ministry of Community and Social Services
Valleyview Centre
I provide parent relief, caring for
an eight-year-old autistic boy.

September 1982
to 1987

Duties:

Ministry of Community and Social Services
Home Provider Program
I provided day care in my home for
five families and took a child care course
through the ministry and received a certificate.

April 1981 to
July 1981
Duties:

Sasha Park Community Centre
Seniors Outreach Worker
I provided a houskeeping service
for seniors.

Figure 7.5 A WEAK RESUME *Why will this person likely be turned down for an interview?*

```
July I980 to        Childrens Aid Society
August I980         Child Care Worker
Duties:             I took care of 3 children ages
                    I3, 9, II, while their mother
                    was undergoing treatment for alcoholism
                    at the New Life Clinic.

Other

May I987            Board of Directors
to present          I have been serving on a founding
                    Board of Directors, working on the
                    development of a housing co- operative.


Excellent referrences upon request.
```

Figure 7.5 A *(Continued)*

```
                              RESUME

                           LISA GIMLICH
           123 Braemar Way,  Forestville, Ontario    K0R 3R5

                            555-9876

EDUCATION

   1988-1990      SOCIAL SERVICE PROGRAM        Waskasoo College
                                               Forestville, Ontario

                  This program covered both theory and practice in
                  counselling, client support, and enabling, including
                  extensive field placement.

   1982-1983      MINI CHILD CARE PROGRAM       Waskasoo College
                                               Forestville, Ontario

                  This 5-month course covered basic Child Care practices
                  and theory and certified me as a Childcare Worker.


FIELD PLACEMENTS

   1989-1990      COUNSELLOR                    Jersey Youth Services
                                               Inner City Youth Program

                  As a counsellor for displaced youth, I handled referrals,
                  I.D. verifications, intakes, group counselling, and some
                  reception.

   January-       CENTRE COORDINATOR            Forestville Volunteer Centre
   May 1989
                  I handled community relations and interviewing, ran a
                  variety of projects including Recognition, Church
                  Outreach, and Recruitment.  I was also responsible for
                  office duties.

EMPLOYMENT

   1989-          CHILDCARE WORKER              Ministry of Community
   Present        (Valleyview Centre)          and Social Services

                  I provide extensive care for an eight year old autistic
                  boy.

   1982-1987      CHILDCARE WORKER              Ministry of Community
                  Home Provider Program        and Social Services

                  I provided ministry-certified home day care for five
                  families.
```

Figure 7.5 B IMPROVED VERSION *What additions have made this resume better than Lisa's first version?*

Lisa Gimlich   2

1981   SENIOR OUTREACH WORKER   Sasha Park Community
                                             Centre

              I provided a housekeeping service for seniors.

1980   CHILDCARE WORKER   Children's Aid Society

              I took over the care of three children, aged 9, 11, and
              13, while their mother underwent treatment for
              alcoholism at the New Life Clinic.

COMMUNITY SERVICE

1987-   BOARD OF DIRECTORS   Allendon Community Association
Present   Founding Member   Forestville, Ontario

              I have participated in a variety of projects, including
              the development of a housing co-operative.

AREAS OF SKILL

    Specialized   I am experienced in therapeutic counselling, client
                   support, group dynamics, and enabling. As well, I am
                   familiar with the procedures and requirements of both
                   the Ministry of Community and Social Services and the
                   Children's Aid Society.

    Personal   I learn quickly, am enthusiastic and dedicated. I am
                   also organized and disciplined, and work effectively to
                   deadlines.

    Interpersonal I have skill in active listening, supportiveness and
                   questioning techniques. I can interact effectively with
                   clients of diverse backgrounds and with other
                   professionals.

Figure 7.5 B *(Continued)*

Our final resume, Pat Hare's (Figure 7.6) is also chronologically organized, but see how Pat has handled his skills area: it is written in paragraphs, but individual skills are boldfaced to make them stand out. He has used boldfacing throughout the document to make it even more readable and easier to follow. Once again, notice the layout of Pat's background; he has not included a career objective because his training has prepared him specifically for one kind of position. Note that on this document, the education, as Pat's most recent experience, comes first.

Pat doesn't have a lot of experience, but he has trained himself in a specific career field, and though he is not widely experienced he will impress an employer with his well-developed and professional resume. It is in such a case that this resume format really comes in handy: Pat's background would appear sketchy indeed if he had merely listed it in a strictly chronological format.

PATRICK MURRAY HARE

PO Box 1234,   Forestville, Ontario   K0B 4L0
(519) **632 2791**

EDUCATION

1990	**Pharmacy Technician**	Waskasoo College Forestville, Ontario

Program covered all aspects of Pharmacy operation, including both laboratory techniques and retail business operations, and included an extensive placement component.

1988	**Grade 12 Diploma**	Forestville High Forestville, Ontario

EMPLOYMENT HISTORY:

1990	**Pharmacy Technician**	Value Drugs Cedarville, Ontario

Duties included assisting the pharmacist in the dispensary, and involved all other aspects of retail pharmacy work. My three-month employment was work experience for the Pharm. Tech. program at Tomahawk College.

Apr. 1985– Aug. 1989	**Clerk/ Stock Person**	IGA Groceteria Forestville, Ontario

This position was part time during school year, and full time during summers. I unpacked and priced stock, maintained shelf inventory, packed orders and assisted customers.

Jun. 1985– Sep. 1985	**General Laborer**	County of Pine Hill Ontario

On construction sites I did painting, shingling, general carpentry, and some demolition.

AREAS OF SKILL:

Technical   As a trained **Pharmacy Technician**, I am familiar with all related **laboratory techniques**, including **aseptic**, **IV admixture**, **TPN**, **compounding**, prepackaging, and **dispensing** techniques, as well as **inventory control** procedures such as ordering/receiving, invoicing, and third-party billing.

Figure 7.6 *Evaluate Pat's resume to show how it displays the qualities of an effective resume: visual appeal and attention to the reader's needs.*

                                                              Pat Hare   2

Personal   In both my education and my previous work experience,
                  I have always shown myself to be an **honest, reliable**
                  worker who takes pride in a job well done. I take an
                  organized approach to my work and perform it to
                  exacting standards. I am able to take **initiative** and
                  work effectively to deadlines.

Interpersonal   I am able to function effectively in a **leadership**
                  role or in **cooperation** with others. I maintain a
                  cheerful outlook and am **flexible** in dealing with
                  other people.

REFERENCES:

    A list of referees is attached.

Figure 7.6 *(Continued)*

The Letter of Application

Types of Application Letters

Like all business correspondence, a job application letter must be clear, concise, cohesive, correct, complete, and courteous.

There are two types of application letters. Both, in a sense, are sales letters; as in the resume, the product is your suitability for the job.

The solicited letter is written in answer to an advertisement for an available position, while the unsolicited letter is written to a firm in the hope that a suitable position is currently, or is about to become, available. The advantage of the second, if your timing is right, is obvious: there will be less competition than for an advertised position.

Both letters perform essentially the same task, however, and may be broken down into steps. How many paragraphs each step takes will depend on the background of the individual and the nature of the job applied for.

Appeal to the Employer!

Remember that the application letter, like all business writing, must be carefully directed to your reader's needs and expectations. What you want to say is not as important as what the employer wants to hear, and what you choose to put into the letter should be conditioned by those reader needs. Ask yourself what questions an employer will want your application to answer. The following steps can serve as a guideline; you could plan to allow one paragraph for each step, though each step may be shorter or longer than a paragraph.

Step 1

The first question an employer will have upon receiving your letter is "What is this about?" You should begin by identifying your reason for writing. In a letter than answers an ad, state the title of the position you are applying for, quoting the competition number if there is one, and the source and date of the advertisement. For an unsolicited letter, state clearly the type of work you desire and enquire whether such a position is currently open or soon to become available. You may wish to use a re- or subject-line for both types of letters, identifying the position sought by title or type.

Step 2

An employer's second question will likely be, "What qualifications does the applicant have for the job?" For both solicited and unsolicited letters, provide the employer with a very brief outline of the highlights of your background and your reasons for applying for this position. This need not be elaborate, since your resume will take care of the details, but should provide some legitimate reason why you would be a suitable candidate for the position. You may in this paragraph refer the employer to your resume, which will be attached.

Step 3

An employer's third concern will be what makes you the best candidate for the job. Here you will want to be specific about why you are more suitable than the other applicants for the position. You may choose some particularly relevant skills and details from your resume, qualifying these with brief examples appropriate to the job you seek. This is where you really sell your own appropriateness for the position; show the employer what you can do for him or her and emphasize your strengths.

Step 4

If you have not yet referred the employer to your resume, do so now; mention also that you have attached letters of recommendation or other documentation (if you have done so) or invite the employer to contact references you have listed.

Step 5

Close with a strong statement of confidence in your abilities; thank the employer for considering you, and ask for an interview. You might say that you will call the employer to set up an interview. This is a good move if you can carry it off. However, if you really can't imagine yourself making such a call, don't say that you will do so. Instead, request an interview at the employer's convenience. Be sure to thank the employer for considering your application, and provide your telephone number where you may be reached or where a message may be left.

Sample Letters of Application

Figures 7.7 and 7.8 are two effective examples of the solicited and the unsolicited application letter.

```
            1324 Main Street
            Red Deer, Alberta
            T4N 2D3

            January 12, 1990


            Ms Nancy Schindelhauer, Manager
            Contemporary Fashions
            1702 Trutch Street
            Vancouver, British Columbia
            V6K 7Y9


            Dear Ms Schindelhauer:

            RE:   Assistant Manager, Red Deer
                  Competition #12-D-465

            Please accept my application for this position in your
            Red Deer store, as advertised in The Edmonton Journal,
            January 11, 1990.  I believe I have the experience you
            are seeking for your new location.

            As my resume explains, I am experienced in customer
            service and stock control and am familiar with most
            aspects of retail operations, including handling cash and
            credit transactions, maintaining stock levels, serving
            customers, and handling complaints and returns.  My work
            as a waitress has also given me experience in dealing
            effectively with client complaints.

            As well, I have completed a course in business-related
            computer programming and have knowledge of basic
            bookkeeping procedures. I am very interested in meeting
            with you to discuss my future with your company, and
            would be available for an interview at your convenience.
            I may be reached at (403) 356 1234

            Sincerely,

            Angela Peterson
            Angela Peterson
```

Figure 7.7 *This solicited letter of application focuses on the employer's needs, making it more likely to be successful.*

PO Box 1234
Forestville, Ontario
K0B 4L0

April 21, 1990

Dr. Donald Dinero, Pharmacist
Value Drugs
34 Center Street
Cedarville, Ontario
K7Y 2F6

Dear Dr. Dinero:

Re: Pharmacy Technician Position

I am a recent graduate of the Pharmacy Technician
Program at Tomohawk College in Forestville, and am very
interested in finding employment in the Cedarville area.
I believe you will find my background of interest if you
are currently looking for an enthusiatic and competent
technician.

I completed the pharmacy program with first class
honors overall, and high marks in all pharmacy-related
courses. The program covers all aspects of retail
pharmacy work, including laboratory and inventory
procedures. As you may already know, the program also
includes a three-month work experience component, which I
spent with Benjamin's Drugs in Forestville. A letter of
recommendation from Dr. Norman Benjamin is attached,
along with a resume of my experience and abilities.

Though I am relatively new to the Pharmacy field, I
am a conscientious and hard-working employee. I am
interested in speaking with you about a possible position
with your firm. I will be available mornings at 632 2791.
Thank you for your consideration.

Yours truly,

Pat Hare

Pat Hare

Figure 7.8 *Notice how Pat emphasizes his relevant experience in his unsolicited letter of application.*

The Application Form

The application form is relatively easy to complete once you have written a resume. Though it may seem unnecessary, some firms require that you submit both a resume and an application form. Some prefer only a form, because it makes comparison between applicants easier. In any case, it's a good idea to know how to complete one.

Forms may vary considerably in their thoroughness. The example I have included below is exhaustive. Though a longer form may seem difficult, it is generally to your advantage because it allows you room to communicate any special skills and abilities which might be overlooked on a shorter form. It can thus help you to make a stronger impression.

In filling out the form below (Figure 7.9), complete all areas as fully as possible, taking special care to fill in areas which ask for elaboration on the form's standard questions. On this form, you will find such areas under the headings "Career Goals" and "Areas of Expertise." It is important to take advantage of these sections, not only because they allow you to distinguish yourself from other applicants, but because one of the most common employer complaints about applicants is failure to fill out forms completely.

The "additional information" questions are especially important; they are areas which you can use to your advantage, elaborating on strengths which may not have shown up clearly in the rest of the application form. Read the enclosed sample carefully and fill in all areas.

APPLICATION FOR EMPLOYMENT

NAME:_____

      (last)   (first)   (middle)

ADDRESS:_____

_____

_____ Phone _____

EMPLOYMENT HISTORY: List in chronoligical order, beginning with most recent and working back.

From   To   Position Held   Name of Firm
_____

    Duties:_____

_____

_____

_____

From   To   Position Held   Name of Firm
_____

    Duties:_____

_____

_____

_____

From   To   Position Held   Name of Firm
_____

    Duties:_____

_____

_____

_____

Figure 7.9 *A typical application form.*

From _____ To _____ Position Held _____ Name of Firm _____

_____

Duties: _____

_____

_____

_____

Do you type? _____ wpm speed _____

Do you drive? _____ Licence class _____

Do you speak French? _____ fluently _____ well _____ some _____

Do you write French? _____ fluently _____ well _____ some _____

Are you computer literate? _____ If yes, explain _____

_____

_____

CAREER GOALS: Briefly describe the nature of the work you are interested in and the origin of this interest:_____

_____

_____

_____

_____

_____

_____

_____

_____

_____

_____

Figure 7.9 *(Continued)*

EDUCATIONAL HISTORY: List in chronoligical order, beginning with most recent and working back.

From	To	Program	Institution	Diploma	Date

Details:

From	To	Program	Institution	Diploma	Date

Details:

From	To	Program	Institution	Diploma	Date

Details:

RELATED ACTIVITIES: Describe any school- or community-related activities in which you have taken part, including offices held:

Figure 7.9 *(Continued)*

AREAS OF EXPERTISE: Elaborate on the above factual material by outlining briefly any skills you have developed from your experiences, any strengths you can bring to your position, or any information not already covered above.

_____

_____

_____

_____

_____

_____

_____

_____

_____

_____

_____

_____

_____

_____

_____

_____

_____

_____

_____

_____

To my knowledge, all of the above information is true and accurate.

Date _____Signature _____

Figure 7.9 *(Continued)*

The Letter of Recommendation

At times, employers will ask for references from people who have known you professionally, either as employers or instructors; sometimes you can simply provide a list of names, but at other times you may need or want to provide a written record of the person's impressions of you.

For a number of reasons it is a good idea to request a letter of recommendation whenever you leave a job or an educational institution. If you apply for a job in an area far away from your previous location, a prospective employer might not be bothered to phone long distance to speak to your referee and may instead hire someone whose references are easier to check. As well, people who have been familiar with your work move on, retire or get promoted, or just plain forget you. A letter written when your performance is current and fresh in the referee's mind is more desirable than a vague recollection written long afterward, which is unlikely to be as enthusiastic.

You should know what a letter of this type should include because you will probably be asking people to write them for you; eventually you may even be writing them for others.

A letter of recommendation is usually written by someone who knows you in an employment or educational context; these two types of reference are considered most appropriate for a job hunt. Most employers prefer them to personal references. However, if for some reason you wish to include a personal letter of reference, it should be written by someone who has some credibility—some status in the community—never by a relative or a buddy. Remember, prospective employers want information regarding your ability to do a job; they will want this information from as reliable a source as possible.

No matter who is writing the letter, the contents of a letter of recommendation are approximately the same. If an employer and referee met face to face, the employer would most likely ask a series of questions about the applicant. The writer of a letter of recommendation, just like any other writer of business letters, should consider the needs of the reader, and provide answers to these most common questions, preferably in this order.

1. How long, and in what context, have I know the person I am writing about? I must indicate my relationship (supervisor? employer? instructor? academic advisor?) to the subject of my letter, and the length of time that I was the person's employer, teacher, or advisor.

2. What is my estimation of this person as an employee or a professional or, if it's an educational reference, as a student? I should provide some specific examples—I might mention grades, work completed, duties of

the position, record of advancement, quality of work, or outstanding achievements.

3. What is my estimation of the subject's personality? Employers want to know what kind of person they are considering for a position. Will he or she get along with others? Is he or she flexible? Cooperative? Personable? Outgoing?

4. Can I make a strong statement of recommendation for the person and invite the employer to contact me for further information? If I can't make a strong recommendation, I should not be writing the letter of recommendation in the first place.

The format for a recommendation letter is like other business letters. Naming the person in a re or subject line will help the reader more easily identify who is described in the letter.

If you ask someone for a recommendation, keep these points in mind.

1. Be sure that the person approached will give you a positive recommendation. Employers expect a very position evaluation in such a letter; a lukewarm or unenthusiastic letter is as bad as a negative evaluation.

2. If the person is unsure of what to say, don't hesitate to make suggestions! Many people are uncertain about what to include in a letter of recommendation and you will want to get as positive a letter as possible. Ask the person to comment upon the three major areas above, and emphasize any qualities which are important to the job you will be seeking.

3. Provide your writer with the correct name and address of the person to whom the letter is addressed, if it is to be sent directly; if not, ask for a general letter addressed "To Whom It May Concern".

The examples below (Figure 7.10 and 7.11) demonstrate effective letters of recommendation.

 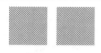

BENJAMIN'S DRUGS

1430 Speedvale Road, Forestville, ON KO7 4I6
(519) 546 4589

April 12, 1990

To Whom It May Concern:

Re: **Patrick Hare**

As pharmacist with Benjamin's Drugs, I had the pleasure
of supervising Pat during his placement from the Pharmacy
Technician program at Waskasoo College.

Throughout his placement period with us, Pat showed
himself to be an interested and diligent worker who
undertook with care all tasks assigned him and completed
them efficiently. He performed well above the recommended
standard for placement students and offered some valuable
suggestions for streamlining our prescription process. I
had not even a moment's concern over Pat's performance of
his duties or his professionalism.

Pat impressed me as a very personable individual who
interacts effectively with customers and staff alike. His
conscientious good humor was appreciated by all who
worked with him, and he made himself a valued member of
the Benjamin's team.

I can without hesitation, therefore, recommend Pat as a
reliable and conscientious employee.

Sincerely,

N. Benjamin

Norman Benjamin (Dr.)
Pharmacist

Figure 7.10 *Note that this letter satisfies the questions an employer is likely to have, and that it supports its claims with examples.*

BEOTHUK COLLEGE

1700 Indian Way, Kamloops, BC V8H 3S6
(604) 123 4523

Mr. Wayne Chiu, Director of Admissions
School of Journalism (Broadcasting)
Tyrrell University
Saskatoon, Saskatchewan
S9R 1F3

April 2, 1989

Dear Mr. Chiu

Re: Duncan Cameron

In response to your letter of March 25, concerning Duncan's application to the School of Journalism, I am happy to provide you with what information I can about his suitability to your program.

I had the pleasure of teaching Duncan in the Radio Broadcasting program here at Beothuk College. I was from the start impressed with Duncan's liveliness and enthusiasm for the business and with his ability to project sincerity and warmth both on-air and off.

I also have a great deal of confidence in his intelligence and mastery of the technical aspects of the business; some of the productions he made for us during his stay here were among the best student work I've encountered in ten years in the program.

My one hesitation, and I add this as a note of caution only, is in regard to Duncan's tendency to suffer anxiety in stressful situations, such as examination periods. This is usually temporary, however, and he invariably gives an outstanding performance anyway. Although I feel that you should be alerted to this tendency, I sincerely do not feel that it will adversely affect Duncan's capacity to do further study in the broadcast area.

In light of my knowledge of Duncan's work and his disposition, I am pleased to endorse him as a suitable candidate for your program.

Sincerely,

Leo Moroni, Chairman
Radio Broadcasting Department

Figure 7.11 *A specific letter of recommendation is addressed to a particular individual, but it covers the same kinds of material as the general letter shown above.*

The Job Interview

If your application has been successful, the employer will be interested in talking with you about the position, and will invite you for an interview. The interview is the employer's chance to get to know you in person, to determine if you are the right person for the job. In the interview, you will want to maintain the positive impression you created with your resume and application.

Remember that the employer's first impression of you strongly influences any decision to hire you. This decision is often made within the first minute of the interview, in the employer's first reaction to you; if this impression is negative, the employer may spend the rest of the interview looking for faults to justify this dislike. It's obviously in your best interest to make the employer's first response to you a positive one. You should do all you can to prepare yourself, and thus give yourself an advantage.

A successful interview, like other effective business communications, depends partly on your preparation; before your interview think carefully about the needs and interests of your audience—the person who may be paying your salary. What does that person want in an employee? What will he or she be looking for?

Although you cannot completely predict the interviewer's response to you, there are three aspects of that initial impression that you can control so as to make it a good one: your appearance, your attitude, and your background knowledge.

Appearance/First Impressions

1. Wear appropriate clothes. For business and professional jobs, you should wear relatively conservative business clothes: a suit is best for both men and women, though for men a sports jacket and dress pants may serve the purpose, and for some jobs a woman may want to wear a dress and jacket. Whatever you wear, avoid splashy colours or wild hairdos, and chunky earrings. If you are applying for a labor or other blue-collar job, dress accordingly; in this situation, a suit might be considered overdressed. No matter what you're wearing, be sure you're neat and clean. Your clothes should be comfortable enough that you don't have to repeatedly adjust or fiddle with them.

2. Be punctual. Arrive at the interview with a few minutes to spare, but not more than fifteen minutes early. Know how long it will take you to arrive by whatever means you're travelling and allow yourself enough time for delays. Be sure to take a watch. Ocasionally, there may be a legitimate reason why you have to be late—car trouble, an accident, illness—if this

happens to you, telephone the person immediately to explain the situation and request a later interview. Don't expect to always be given a second chance, however; frequently no time will be available. Sleeping in or misjudging how long it takes to get to the interview are not acceptable reasons for being late. Even legitimate lateness may create a negative impression that damages your chances, so be on time.

3. Go alone to the interview. An interview is a business meeting, not a social event, and bringing someone with you will cause the interviewer to question your maturity and your awareness of appropriate professional behavior. A confident applicant is more likely to get the job, and you won't look confident if you bring someone else along.

4. When you shake hands, use a firm, confident grip. Don't let your hand hang loosely, but be sure not to grip too tightly either.

5. Don't chew gum or smoke, though the interviewer may do either. If the interviewer smokes, don't do so unless you are invited to. Even then you may wish to refuse. And if you smoke, don't hurriedly take a final puff before going in to the interview. Smokers are usually unaware of it, but non-smoking interviewers can be put off by the reek of second-hand smoke on a candidate.

6. Make eye contact while you speak. Though some people avoid eye contact simply because they are nervous, this habit can make a very negative impression on an interviewer. It can suggest uncertainty or even dishonesty, neither of which will further your chances. Don't avoid meeting the interviewer's eyes or stare at the floor or ceiling.

7. Speak clearly and use correct grammar. Employers do judge applicants' intelligence and education by the way they speak and poor grammar is one of the indicators of weaknesses in either of these areas. Avoid such pitfalls as "I seen," "I done," or "between you and I," and keep away from slang expressions.

8. Watch your body language. Sit comfortably without slumping in your chair or hooking your feet around the chair legs. Don't fidget, tap your fingers, or fiddle with your clothes. You should appear controlled and any of these is a clear message that you are nervous or inexperienced. If you are carrying supporting materials in a case, place it on the floor beside you rather than in the way on the desk. Don't block your view of the employer or the employer's of you, with a large briefcase or other unnecessary props.

Attitude

Many interviewers agree that a good attitude is one of the most important things an applicant can bring to the interview. You should appear confident and positive, but not arrogant. Although you will most likely feel, and the employer will expect, a little nervousness, you should try to be as relaxed and comfortable as you can. Be yourself—at your very best.

1. Avoid bragging or overstating your abilities. Employers, like everyone else, dislike arrogance. Be alert and attentive to questions, enthusiastic and sincere in your answers. Show a willingness to learn and grow with the company; no matter how much you feel you already know, there is always something else to learn.

2. Avoid one-word responses. At the same time, don't take over the interview with long, impossibly complicated replies. Watch the interviewer for cues to tell you when to stop speaking.

3. Show some interest in the company and don't be vague about what you want from your career. Employers like someone who has thought about his or her future, and can show some direction. Indicate a willingness to work hard and start at a reasonable level. You may display ambition, but don't give the impression that you expect to run the company.

4. Don't appear obsessed with money, benefits, or vacations. Don't stress how you can benefit from the position, or how much you need it. Remember that the goal of the interviewer is to find out what you can do for the company, not to hear what it can do for you.

5. Be courteous at all times. Don't do or say anything that could be considered rude or discourteous. Remember this especially when you enter and are met by a receptionist or secretary: rudeness to these people can cost you the job offer, since they often are part of the screening process. Among other things, the employer wants to know how well you will get along with other people in the company, and one measure of this is how you treat the receptionists. Always remember that first impressions count!

Knowledge

Employers are interested in discovering just how well you know the duties of the position you've applied for; they will want you to demonstrate the skill that you have claimed on your resume. You should naturally be prepared to discuss your experience, always remembering to show how it is relevant to the position you are looking for.

But there's much more on the employer's mind. Although primarily interested in what you know about the duties of the job, your prospective employer will be impressed if you can demonstrate knowledge of the company. Try to learn as much as you can about the firm before the interview, for example, how large it is and what products or services it offers. You can find out a little about the company by looking in your local library or checking with the Chamber of Commerce. Here are some questions you might consider answering for yourself before the interview:

1. What is the exact nature of the business—what do they make or do?

2. Is it a local company or is it a branch office/plant?

3. How extensive is their business?

4. How long has the company been in business?

5. What is their management style?

An annual report will give you this information and more that might be useful. If you know someone who works for the company, try to talk to that person. Find out as much as you can. Though you may not be asked such questions in the interview, the more you know when you go in, the more confident you will be and the better impression you will make.

Employers' Questions

Employers also want some indication that you are self-aware, that you know yourself and have thought about your goals, and that you have realistic expectations. They will also be interested to see if you can effectively solve the problems you are likely to face on the job. They will try to determine this information through careful questioning. Though every interview is different, and interviewers have different focuses, there are some questions which occur regularly in one form or another. If you think about these before you go to any interview, and know more or less what you would answer, you will have a better chance of handling the questions effectively. You should try to tailor your answer to fit the job you're applying for, but you should not alter your responses so much that you try to be something you're not. Answer fully and sincerely. Here are some samples of favorite employer questions, with suggestions for answering them.

1. Tell me about yourself. Employers often like to begin the interview with this one, because it not only provides information about you but also shows something of your priorities. What you choose to discuss will tell them what you think is important. Be aware that the employer is

interested primarily in information relevant to the position you've app-lied for. Avoid the temptation to deliver the epic of your life. A brief summary of education and employment highlights, as they have prepa-red you for the job in question, will work best here.

2. What are your strengths? Don't be falsely modest. A mature person knows what his or her strong points are and can state them briefly without either bragging or understating them. Take some time to identify the things you do really well; go back over the skills section of your resume and be ready with some examples.

3. What are your weaknesses? We all have weaknesses, and a mature adult is aware of his or her own. However, be careful when you're answering this question. Don't identify weaknesses in such a way that they are likely to make an employer think twice about hiring you: such comments as "I never finish what I start" or "I'm a kleptomaniac" won't endear you to an employer. If you have such weaknesses, of course you should be trying to correct them, but an interview is not the place to highlight them. Identify weaknesses which show you are human, but not ones which will reveal you as unemployable. For example, you might (if this is true) tell the employer something like "I sometimes take my work too seriously, and don't leave myself enough time for leisure." Or you may identify a not-so-serious flaw and immediately balance it with a positive: "I sometimes don't take criticism well, but I usually use it to correct my weaknesses." Avoid really serious or negative traits, but don't say "I don't have any weaknesses" or "I don't know," and above all make sure you are sincere in your answers. An experienced intervi-ewer can recognize phony or insincere answers and will reject the applicant.

4. Why do you want to work for this company? or Why do you want this job? Your research into the company will give you some information to use here; don't, however, identify pay or benefits as a primary reason for choosing this company. Emphasize the position itself, and don't, as an acquaintance of mine did, answer by saying "because I'm unem-ployed." Employers want some evidence that they are getting the best, not merely the most desperate, applicant. This question might also appear as "What do you think you can do for this company?" accompa-nied by "What can we do for you?" You can best prepare for these questions by thinking them through beforehand and planning how you will answer. Don't memorize an answer though; it is bound to sound false or insincere.

5. What made you choose _____ as a career? There are many acceptable answers to this question, and you will have to choose your own. However, "My father [or mother] is a _____," is not

one of them, nor is "I knew I'd earn lots of money." The employer wants to know that you've made a thoughtful choice, not just an expedient one.

6. What was your favorite subject in college/university/school? You may wish to identify one or two subjects, but watch out for the other half of this question, which asks you to identify the subject(s) you disliked. You may indicate that there were some subjects you liked better than others, but you should avoid sounding like a complainer. Instead of identifying courses you "couldn't stand," indicate that you learned something from all of them, even the ones you didn't particularly enjoy.

7. How would your friends describe you? This is another way for an employer to find out a bit about your self-awareness. You should not be overly modest. Again, try to identify real strengths, but don't sound arrogant.

8. What would you like to be doing in five years? ten? Employers can find out how much thought you've given to your career with this question. They may also be looking for evidence of a commitment to the company. If you say that you're not planning to stay in this job, or in this field, an employer may not want to spend the time or money on training you for the position. Answering "I don't know" isn't a good idea either; an employer might consider it a sign of indecision or immaturity and it could cost you the job. Try to show that you have given some thought to the future, but that you are flexible and able to adjust your goals as well.

9. Do you have plans to further your education? Would you be interested in doing so? Your answer here could depend on whether the employer is wondering if you're open to more training, or afraid you'll quit the job in six months to return to full time study. You should never close any door on yourself. You could indicate that you are willing to take further training if necessary. Even if you don't think right now that you would ever go back to school, remember that with time you might change your mind. On the other hand, you might also want to reassure the employer that you're not going to quit to return to school.

10. One type of question that is often favored by employers is the situation question. The most common type is one in which the interviewer gives an example of an incident which might happen to you in the job, and asks for your solution. There isn't any way to prepare for this question; it's designed to test your awareness of the job's requirements. You might try going over your experience in your memory. Think of difficult situations you have faced and how you handled them; analyze how you might have handled them better than you did. If you expect such a question, and think about how you might answer it, you will be better

prepared for it. The question may also appear in another form, such as

>Give me an example of a situation in which you showed leadership.
>
>Tell me about a situation in which you resolved a difficulty.
>
>Tell me about a situation in which you initiated change.
>
>Tell me about a situation in which you handled criticism.
>
>Describe an achievement you are proud of.

11. These questions might also be phrased evaluatively. Instead of asking for an example, the interviewer might simply ask you to outline your capabilities using such questions as:

>How well do you handle pressure?
>
>How do you handle criticism?
>
>Are you able to handle change?

You may wish to support your answer with an example from your work or educational experience.

12. The employer might also probe your attitude toward others with such questions as:

>Are you usually right?
>
>Are other people's ideas as important as yours?

Of course, you will want to show some openness to others' views and not indicate that you believe only you are ever correct. Provide some balance in your answer: you're not always right, naturally, but you are not always wrong either. You must show that you are capable of making decisions, but that you can also recognize good ideas that others put forward and that you can compromise.

>Do you make mistakes?
>
>How do you handle those?
>
>Can you give me an example?

Naturally you will want to show that you are aware that you can make mistakes, but also that you can learn from them. If you say you do not make mistakes, the interviewer will reject you outright, because of course we all make errors from time to time, and the measure of us is in how we handle the errors we make.

13. You might also be asked: How would you describe a good (teacher, electrician, engineer) _____? What makes you a good (teacher, electrician, engineer) _____? An acquaintance of mine once answered the latter question with "I don't know; I just do it!" By now, of course, you know that's not an appropriate answer; a good answer should be thought out beforehand in a way that's relevant to your program or profession.

In answering any of these questions, keep in mind the probable needs and interests of all employers: they will be looking for someone who is confident and capable, but not arrogant or self-absorbed. Admit to mistakes, but show that you have learned from them and handle criticism effectively. Be honest and not overly modest; be confident but not arrogant. Show that you have both strengths and weaknesses, but that your weaknesses are not serious and can be overcome. Don't cite weaknesses which are likely to damage your employment chances.

Some Reasons Why People Don't Get Hired

Of course, there are many of these, some of which you may not be able to control; however, there are some elements that you can control. These are some of the reasons employers have given for turning down applicants:

Late to the interview
Dressed inappropriately
Seemed unduly nervous
Fidgeted; did not appear relaxed or confident
Didn't answer questions fully; rambled on too long
Attempted to dominate interview
Was arrogant or self-important
Criticized former employers
Appeared more interested in pay and benefits than in work
Chewed gum
Was unable or unwilling to provide references
Spoke poorly, with poor grammar or diction
Handshake was limp
Knew nothing about the company
Had exaggerated on the application or resume
Had ambitions far beyond abilities
Had no clear goals or professional interests
Appeared whiny or unmotivated
Could not admit to weaknesses or mistakes; tended to blame others
Was defensive when answering questions
Unwilling to start at the bottom
Lacked courtesy, was rude or ill-mannered
Poor school record
Appeared insincere or glib
Lied on the application or resume

What to Expect

Interviews can vary not only in the type and number of questions that employers ask, but in other ways as well. There is no set pattern for interviews and no right way to conduct them in terms of length or number of screenings. Employers tend to decide for themselves what selection process best suits their needs, and the more interviews you go to the greater variety you will see.

For example, the length of time you spend in an interview may be anywhere from twenty minutes to two or even three hours, depending on the type of position and the number of applicants. (An acquaintance of mine recently attended an interview which lasted seven hours!) Often the person who telephones you to set up in the interview will indicate how long it will take; if she or he doesn't do so, allow yourself two hours, just to be safe.

You may be interviewed by one person, by two or three together, or even by a committee of five or more. Again, you may be told this ahead of time. But whether you are told or not, be prepared; the more responsible the position, the more likely there will be more than one interviewer. In some companies or institutions, two or three people interview you separately, then compare impressions. This may be done on the same day (you may spend twenty to forty minutes with three different people successively) or on subsequent days. This is neither a good nor a bad sign; it merely shows the employer's personal preference.

In any of these cases, don't be thrown off by interviewers taking notes while you speak. Remember that they have seen several different people in a short space of time and are merely interested in keeping track of what was said. It's really for your benefit—you wouldn't want an interviewer to forget your brilliant answers, would you?

Sometimes, depending on the employer and on the position, you may be asked to complete some form of testing. Occasionally these tests will be vocationally specific—secretarial applicants may have to take a typing test, drivers may be asked to operate a vehicle, or trainers may have to give a sample lesson. In these cases, the interviewer is interested in knowing that you really do have the level of skill needed for the job.

But there are other kinds of tests that you may be asked to take, and these you can't really prepare yourself for; these tests are thought to reveal your general intelligence, attitude, and/or aptitude for the position you are interested in. Not all employers use such tests, but those who do really believe in their usefulness. Your best bet if you are asked to write these is to be as honest and forthright as you can. Most of the tests are designed to double-check your responses by asking several questions aimed at the same information, so keep in mind that it's difficult to try to second-guess the tests. Fudged answers can usually be identified by the cross-questions.

Simply try to relax as much as possible and do your best. There is nothing to be frightened of, and you will do better if you can keep from being too upset.

There is much talk these days about poor writing skills among college and university graduates, and many employers have expressed concern over such weaknesses. As a result, occasionally an employer will ask applicants to write a piece of business correspondence—a letter or a memo—right on the spot, in response to a situation such as the ones given in the chapter on letters and memos. You should be prepared to write if necessary; you might review the chapters on the business letter and the memo before you go to the interview. In this case, the employer will be looking not only for proper letter or memo format but more importantly for correct grammar and sentence structure, and the other Six C's of business writing.

Problem Questions

Employers are no longer permitted to ask an applicant questions which will solicit information about age, marital status, religious affiliation, ethnic background, or family relationships. It is illegal to do so, but occasionally you will encounter an interviewer who asks you such questions anyway, either because of inexperience or because of deliberate disregard for the rules. You are obviously not obliged to answer such questions, but refusing to do so could sometimes cost you the position.

The decision to answer such queries or not is a very personal one, based on your own comfort level. If a question about marital status, for example, is not a problem for you, you may wish to answer even though, strictly speaking, it's not really appropriate. You will sometimes be able to determine the employer's train of thought from the context of the remark. An employer may really be thinking about overtime, and ask about your marital status because he or she feels overtime might be more difficult for a married person. You may choose to rephrase the question in your response, in order to speak directly to the employer's concern. For example, a prospective employer may ask if you are married. You could answer: "If you're concerned about my willingness to work overtime, I am willing to put in all the time the job requires."

If, on the other hand, the interviewer's questions seem a bit too personal or make you very uncomfortable, you may wish to decline to answer. Doing so is tricky, though. If you simply refuse, saying that you don't see the relevance of the question to the job, you will probably turn the interviewer against you. You may try restating the question as in the example, but you should be prepared to balance your need for the job against your willingness to answer inappropriate questions. This is entirely a judgement call, and it's important to know for yourself how much is too much. Most interviewers want to see you at your best, and will try very hard to put you at ease. However, if you do run into a difficult situation, know how much of such behavior is tolerable to you, and don't be afraid to leave if you have to. If the interview is that unpleasant, it's unlikely that you would want to work for this company anyway.

Interviewing, like everything else in this book, is a skill you can learn and polish. You can do this best by practising. Go to as many interviews as you can, even if you're not sure you would want the job. You can never get too much experience, and every interview you go to will make the next one easier.

THINGS TO TRY

1. Write your own Job Package, including a complete application letter, a resume of your experience and education, a completed job application form, and a letter of recommendation.

   Letter of Application: Use the job descriptions provided by your instructor or answer an ad from your local newspaper. Type the letter in one of the formats you've learned.

   Resume: You may complete this as though you have finished your current year of study. Review the section on resume writing in this chapter and remember that it must be correct, legible, and clear.

   Application Form: There is an application form on page 173. Photocopy it and fill it out completely in ink (or type). Be sure to sign it.

   Recommendation Letter: Pretending to be a former employer or instructor, write a letter recommending yourself for this job.

2. You work for the Public Relations department of Communications Corporation. Your boss, Toby Trapper, has struck a hiring committee in your department for a position advertised as follows in the paper:

ADMINISTRATIVE ASSISTANT
PUBLIC RELATIONS

Major corporation in the Communications field seeks an administrative assistant for its public relations department. Primary duties will include writing correspondence to other communications leaders and the general public, as well as some general office duties.

The successful applicant will have:
— superior writing/composition ability, with thorough knowledge of techniques of business writing
— good interpersonal skills
— ability to work without supervision
— strong organizational ability
— keyboarding speed of 40wpm
— pleasant telephone manner

Experience in a secretarial position would be considered an asset, but is not the most important qualification for this position. Applicants with strong, demonstrated skills in communications, particularly writing, will be considered for training.

Submit resumes in confidence to:

Julie Fitzgerald, Personnel Manager
Communications Corporation
555 California Street
Vancouver, British Columbia
V1R 7H9

The initial screening has been done by Julie Fitzgerald's department. It is up to your committee to make the final decision from the resumes she has forwarded. You should look at the sample resumes in this chapter, and then evaluate the following submissions (Figures 7.13 to 7.18) according to the criteria you have learned. See if you can identify specific weaknesses of these resumes and letters in terms of content, format, and style. Have they clearly identified purpose and placed the reader's needs first? Make a list of the weaknesses you have found and compare them with those identified by your classmates or instructor.

15 Cedar Avenue
Greyfowl, BC
V8G J9K

Dear Sir:

Enclosed please find a copy of my resume for your
perusal. I have experience as a secretary.

I look forward to hearing from you at your earliest
convenience.

Sincerely,

Leola Burdett

Leola Burdett

Figure 7.12 *The application letter is meant to encourage an employer to read the attached resume. What impression does Leola Burdett's letter make on you?*

```
                              - 1 -

                    RESUME - LEOLA BURDETT


ADDRESS:      15 Cedar Avenue        SIN: 987 654 321
              Greyfowl, BC
              V8G J9K

PHONE:        678 9087


PREVIOUS WORK EXPERIENCE:

--      Clerk Typist Position at British Columbia Social
        Services for a temporary 6 months. From September/
        89 to February/90
        Supervisor: Greta Grey  Phone: 234 5678 (8:15 -
        4:30 p.m.)


--      Bartender/Waitress at "Steer's Neighborhood Pub".
        Worked from April/89 to September/89
        Supervisor: Dave Pickard  Phone: hm 123-2234
        wk 345-2876

--      Various Waitress positions in Swan Valley, BC,
        between the period of 1984 to 1988. Along with
        cashier positions also.

--      Volunteer at St. John's Hospital in Swan Valley,
        BC. In the Geriatric ward.


EDUCATION:

--      Attended Northeastern High School in Strickland, BC
        as a Adult Student for a grade 12 general diploma.
        (1988)

--      Correspondence Course for a Medical Receptionist
        Diploma through Drucker Career Training Centre
        situated in Vancouver, BC.

--      General courses taken in high school were: Office
        Procedures, Typing (3 yrs.), English, Business
        Education and also Accounting.
```

Figure 7.13 *Compare this resume to the advertisement for the position. How well has Leola targeted her resume to the job she wants?*

```
                              - 2 -

        PERSONAL INFORMATION:

        BIRTHDATE:  15/05/68

        STATUS:  Single Parent


        SKILLS & KNOLEDGE:

        --      Typing at 50 w.p.m.

        --      Ability to operate all office machines in general.

        --      Can operate a Word Processor and a dicta-phone
                machine.
        --      S
        --      Spelling/75% average, Math/75% average.

        --      Know most aspects of bartending and barmaiding.

        --      Handle cash well, change register tapes and do
                cash-outs.


        EXTRACURRICULAR ACTIVITIES:

        --      Presently enjoy all indoor and outdoor sports and
                activities.

        REFERENCES:

        --      Dave Pickard    Phone: 123-2234 (hm)   345-2876 (wk)

        --      Linda Crumb     Phone: 453-9876 (hm)   219-0987 (wk)

        --      Denise Gorland Phone: 573-0287 (hm)

        --      Mrs. Roest      Phone: 2               938-3847 (wk)
```

Figure 7.13 *(Continued)*

1990 03 10

Julie Fitzgerald, Personnel Manager
Communications Corporation
555 California Street
Vancouver, British Columbia
V1R 7H9

Dear Ms. Fitzgerald:

Please be advised that I am interested in the position of

Administrative Assistant at your firm in Vancouver.

Enclosed is my resume documenting my experience and

education.

Yours truly,

Glenda MacDougall

Glenda MacDougall

Figure 7.14 *Evaluate Glenda MacDougall's letter using the criteria you have learned for business letter format and application letter style.*

Glenda MacDougall

5555-44 Street, Westock, New Brunswick
E4F 2R5
Res. (987) 345 7896
Bus. (987) 344 1230

History

November 1988 to Present	Personal Secretary to District Agriculturist, New Brunswick Agriculture, Westock, New Brunswick
July/August 1989	Attended Sproxler H.S., Saint John to obtain Grade 12 English
February 1986	Administrative officer, Tartan River Further Education Council, Box 980, Tartan River, New Brunswick - worked out of own home - planned and directed all phases of Council business - received and processed all correspondence - prepared copy and arranged for printing of twice-yearly, twelve-page advertising brochure - prepared financial reports, payroll for 40 instructors, accounts receivable and payable and bookkeeping - taking and transcribing minutes of general and executive meetings - set up and maintained filing system - worked independently at all times - attended seminars and workshops re position
June 1983 to January 1986	Owner-Manager of retail fabric store, "Sew-You-See", Tartan River, New Brunswick
March 1979 to May 1983	Clerk-Stenographer, Quinpool College, Tartan River, New Brunswick
July 1976 to August 1981	Secretary to Regional Manager, Agricultural Development Corporation, New Brunswick Agriculture, Tartan River, New Brunswick

Figure 7.15 *Check the job requirements listed in the advertisement. How well has Glenda addressed the needs of her potential employer?*

February 1971 September 1977	Secretary to Regional Manager, Dairy Specialist and Regional Livestock Specialist, New Brunswick Agriculture, Tartan River, New Brunswick.
February 1973	Graduated from Keystone Secretarial School with Business diploma, Eastlock College, Eastlock, N.B.
June 1972	Graduated from High School with Commercial diploma from Tartan High School, Tartan River, New Brunswick
Volunteer Work	Elected to Post Secondary Education committee for Westock -council to investigate development of community college in Westock
Personal Infomation	Married - three children, two living at home Birth date - February 2, 1951

References available upon request

Figure 7.15 *(Continued)*

General Delivery
Brookfield, Alberta
T0M 9I9

March 11, 1990

Julie Fitzgerald, Personnel Manager
Communications Corporation
555 California Street
Vancouver, British Columbia
V1R 7H9

Dear Ms. Fitzgerald:

                Re: Administrative Assistant Position

I am a recent graduate of the Secretarial Science program
at Modern City College in Modern City, and am very
interested in relocating to the Vancouver area; I would
like to be considered for this position, advertised in
the Edmonton Journal.

I completed the Secretarial program with first class
honors, achieving top marks in office management and
writing courses. The program provided experience in a
variety of skills related to successful office
operations, including a model office experience component
in which I was particularly successful.

An intensive course in business writing, covering memos,
letters, reports, proposals, and promotional writing is
also part of the program. I earned grades of 9 (+90%) in
all courses involving major writing components, and have
been commended for my organized and disciplined approach
to my work.

You will find me thorough, conscientious, and committed
to producing high-quality written work. I am very
interested in joining Communications Corporation, and
look forward to speaking with you about this attractive
career opportunity. I will be available at (403) 555 5106
mornings. Thank you for your consideration.

                        Yours truly,

                        Marlene Dell

                        Marlene Dell

Figure 7.16 *Evaluate this letter for content and format. How effective will it be in meeting the employer's needs?*

```
                         RESUME

                      MARLENE DELL

          HOME ADDRESS:  General Delivery
                         Brookfield, Alberta
                         T0M 9I9
                         (403) 555 5106

CAREER OBJECTIVE:

               After several years raising a family, I have
               prepared myself for a career Secretarial
               Science. I am primarily interested in employment
               as an administrative assistant in a setting
               where my life skills as well as my specialized
               training will be of most benefit.


EDUCATION:

  Sept. 1988-    Secretarial    Modern City College
  April 1990     Science        Modern City, Alberta

               The program covered all aspects of Secretarial
               Science including office procedures, machine
               transcription, typing and data processing, as
               well as written and interpersonal communication
               and public speaking.

               The course also included hands-on
               experience in a model office situation.

  May 1988 -     High School    Modern City College
  Aug. 1988      Equivalency    Modern City, Alberta

               In order to round out my High School courses and
               prepare myself for entry to the Secretarial
               Program, I completed English, Business Math, and
               Social Studies.

EMPLOYMENT HISTORY:

  Nov. 1987 -    Resort         Coyote River Golf Resort
  Apr. 1988      Worker         Coyote River, Alberta

               As occasional help, I assisted in the running of
               the resort, handling a variety of duties from
               customer service and banquest set-up to
               convention bookings.
```

Figure 7.17 *Considering the qualities that your firm is looking for, how effectively has Marlene Dell focused on the job requirements?*

Marlene Dell 2

| Jun. 1980 | Partner/ | Morton Janitorial Service |
| Jun. 1984 | Manager | Brookfield, Alberta |

Under contract with Alberta Natural Gas Ltd., I operated a successful janitorial service with one other individual. Our business was so successful that we won additional contracts and hired additional staff to meet the demand. I handled all aspects of the cleaning business, including training new staff.

AREAS OF SKILL:

Technical

As a trained secretary, I am familiar with related office procedures and techniques, including typing, filing, and reception, as well as business procedures such as ordering/ receiving, invoicing, accounting and third-party billing. I can type accurately (50 wpm), operate a computer terminal, and write clearly and effectively.

Personal

I am an honest and meticulous worker and strive to do my best whatever the task. I am organized and punctual and work hard to meet deadlines. I am also able to assume responsibility when necessary to get the job done.

Interpersonal

I genuinely like people and am able to interact effectively in cooperation with others; I maintain a cheerful outlook and am flexible in my approach to situations. I understand that people are sometimes difficult to handle and am able to show tact and patience in my dealings with them.

REFEREES:

Mrs. D. Malvolio   Coyote River Golf Resort
Owner/Manager   PO Box 1378
                    Brookfield, Alberta
(403) 555 6050   TOC 2H0

Ms. Maureen Vapid   Modern City College
Secretarial   PO Box 5005
                    Modern City, Alberta
(403) 342 3286   T4W 5K5

Figure 7.17 *(Continued)*

Index

Accident report. *See* Incident report
Accuracy. *See* Correctness
Acknowledgement letters, 29
    sample, 30
Active and passive voice, 30
Analytical report, 66
Analytical resume, 134
Application
    form, 172
        sample, 174–176
    letter of, 168
        samples, 170–171
Addresses
    inside, 38
    return, 38
Appearance
    of business letters, 7
    in job interviews, 181
    in oral reports, 121
    of reports. *See* Format
Appendices, 64, 88
Appendix. *See* Appendices
Audience. *See also* Reader
    in business writing, 14
    employer as, 168
    in oral presentations, 119
    in reports, 68

Bad news letters, 29
Bibliography, 88
Body. *See* Discussion

Business letters, 27–55. *See also* Letters
Business writing planner, 15

Career objective, in resumes, 134
Chronological resume, 134
Clarity, 1, 6
Clausal modifiers, 18
Clichés, 6, 11, 16
Closed punctuation, 45–46
Closing, 39
Coherence. *See* Cohesiveness
Cohesiveness, 6
Complaint letters, 31
Complimentary closing, 39
Communication
    deciding what to communicate, 27–36
    importance of, 1
    tone in, 7
Completeness, 7, 9
Conciseness, 6
Conclusion, 3
    of formal reports, 88
    of informal reports, 64
Congratulations, letter of, 29
    sample, 30
Connectives, 6
Copy notation, 40
Correctness, 7
Courtesy, 7
Covering letter, *See* Letter of application
Crossover resume, 134

Date, in letters and memos
    line in memo, 41
    numerical styles, 38
    writen form, 38
Delivering an oral presentation, 121
Diagram. *See* Illustrations
Discussion
    of formal report, 88
    of informal report, 63
    of letters and memos, 3, 39, 42
Drawing. *See* Illustrations
Dress
    in interviews, 181, 188
    in oral reports, 121–122

Editing, 14–19
    assignments, 20–25
Education, in resumes, 136
Employment application. *See* Job application
Employment experience, in resumes, 137
Enclosure notations, 40
Evaluation report, 66
Experience, in resumes, 137
Extemporaneous speech, 121
Eye contact, 122

Formal reports. *See also* Informal reports
    appendix, 64, 88
    assignments, 113
    bibliography, 88
    choosing a format, 68
    conclusion, 88
    cover, 87
    discussion, 63
    introduction, 87
    letter of transfer/transmittal, 87
    planning, 67
    proposals, 67, 94
    sample formal report, 97
    summary, 1, 63, 87
    table of contents, 87
    title page, 87
    visuals, 89–96
Forms
    application, 173–176
    business writing planner, 15
    performance appraisal, 70

    report writing planner, 65
"From" line of memo, 41
Front matter of formal reports
    letter of transfer/transmittal, 87
    summary, 63, 81
    table of contents, 87
    title page, 87
Full block style, 44, 45
Functional resume, 134

Gestures, in oral presentations, 122
Good news letters, 140
Graphs, 92

Illustrations, in formal reports, 89–96
Impromptu speeches, 120
Incident report, 66
Informal reports
    accident. *See* Incident
    appendix, 80
    assignments, 80
    conclusion, 64
    discussion, 63
    evaluation, 66
        sample form, 70
    format
        memo or business letter, 67
        choosing a format, 68
    forms, 69
        sample, 70–71
    headings, 72
    incident, 66
    investigative, 66
    occurrence, 66
    organization, 72
    parts, 63, 72
    periodic, 66
    planning, 65
    progress, 66
    proposal, 67
    sample informal report, 72, 76
    semiformal, 74
        contents, 75
        sample, 78
    styles, 67
    types. *See* styles

Inside address, 38
Interview. *See* Job Interview
Introduction
    of formal report, 87
    of informal report, 63
Investigative report, 66

Job application
    application form, 172
        sample, 173–176
    application letter, 168
        samples, 170–171
    recommendation letter, 177
        contents, 177–178
        samples, 179–180
    resume, 133–145
Job interview
    attitude, 183
    first impression, 181
    knowledge, 183
    problem questions, 190
    typical questions, 184–188
    what to expect, 189
    what to wear, 181
    why people don't get hired, 188
Job search. *See* Job application

Layout, 9
Length, in resumes, 144
Letters
    acknowledgement, 29
    application, 168
    assignments, 50
    body, 39
    closing, 39
    company letterhead, 38
    company name, 39
    complaint, 31
        sample, 32
    contents, 27–36
    congratulation, 29
    date, 38
    file numbers, 41
    format, 44
    full block, 44, 45
    inside address, 38
    layout, 9, 11

    modified semiblock, 44, 47
    notations, 40
    parts, 36
    re or subject line, 39
    reader's name, 38–39
    recommendation, 177
    refusal, 34
        sample, 37
    request, 28
    reply, 28
    return address, 38
    sales, 33
    salutation, 38
    samples, 32, 37, 45–47
    secretary's notation, 40
    semiblock, 44, 46
    transmittal, 87
    types, 44–47
Line drawings. *See* Illustrations
Lists, for emphasis, 19
Linking words. *See* Connectives

Main point, 3, 14, 16, 62
Memos. *See also* Letters
    assignments, 56
    body, 42
    contents, 27–36
    date, 41
    format, 41, 44, 48, 49
    notations, 41
    parts, 41
    when to write, 27, 42
Modified semiblock style, 44, 47

Numerical dates, 38

Occurrence reports, 66
Open Punctuation, 45
Oral presentations
    audible factors, 123
    audience, 119, 127
    assignments, 132
    briefing, 127
    choosing a topic, 125
    context, 120, 128
    delivery, 121
    dress, 121

enunciation, 123
extemporaneous, 121
eye contact, 122
facial expressions, 122
gestures, 122
impromptu, 120
manuscript, 120
memorized, 120
notecard, 126
pacing, 124
pitch, 123
practice, 130
preparation, 124
purpose, 119, 127
sample notecard, 126, 128
tone, 126
types, 120
visible factors, 121
visual aids, 123, 129
volume, 123

Passive voice, 17
Periodic reports, 66
Personal information
    in resumes, 135
Personal titles, 40
Performance appraisal. *See* Evaluative reports
Persuasive writing
    hard sell, 34
    proposals, 94
    sales letters, 33
Photographs. *See* Illustrations
Pie charts. *See* Illustrations
Planning
    business letters and memos, 15
    oral reports, 124
    reports, 67
Progress reports, 66
Proposals, 67, 94
    sample, 97
Punctuation, of letters, 44–45
Purpose, 4, 119

Questions, in job interview
    problem, 190
    typical, 184–188

"Re" line
    in letters, 39
    in memos, 42
Reader
    expectations, 5
    identifying your, 4, 14
    knowledge, 5
    needs, 5
Recommendation
    in formal reports, 64
    in informal reports, 64
    letters of, 177
References, job search, 140, 177
Refusal, letters of, 34
Repetition, 18
Reports
    analytical, 66
    appendices, 64, 88
    bibliography, 88
    charts, 94
    conclusion, 64, 88
    discussion, 63, 88
    editing, 27–36
    formal, 86–113
    front matter, 87
    graphs, 92
    headings, 89
    illustrations, 90
    incident, 66
    informal, 62–85
    investigative, 66
    memo or letter format, 67
    occurrence, 66
    oral, 119–132
    organization, 72, 75
    parts, 62–65, 86–88
    planner, 65
    recommendations, 64, 88
    summary, 63, 87
    table of contents, 87
Request
    letters, 27
    reasonableness of, 28
Response letters, 28
Resume. *See also* Job application
    achievements, 138

analytical, 134
awards, 136
community service, 138
contents, 135–140
crossover, 134
education, 136
employment history, 137
format, 140–143
functional, 134
layout. *See* format
parts, 135–140
samples, 145–167
skills, 138
    interpersonal, 139
    practical, 139
    specialized, 139
types, 134
volunteer work, 137
Return address, 38
Revising, 16–19

Sales letters, 33
Salutation of letters, 38
Secretary's notations, 40
Semiformal reports. *See* Informal reports
Signature, in letters and memos, 40, 42
Six C's, 5, 14, 28, 62, 75, 107, 115
Skills, in resumes, 138–139

Speeches. *See* Oral presentations
Subject line. *See* "Re" line
Summary
    in business writing, 1
    in reports, 63, 87

Table of contents, in formal reports, 87
Title
    of formal report, 87
    job or position, 135, 168
    personal, 40
"To" line in memo, 41
Tone, 7, 8, 29, 33, 34, 36, 42
Transitional words. *See* Connnectives
Typist's notations. *See* Notations

Visual. *See also* Layout, Illustrations
    appeal in letters and memos, 3, 7
    appeal in resumes, 140–143
    in oral presentations, 121
    use in formal reports, 89–96
Voice, of verbs, 17

White space, 3, 140
Writing Style, 14–19
Wordiness. *See also* Conciseness, 6, 18
    exercise, 20